ROGER STEVE
APRIL, 1990

Suncell

SUNCELL

Energy, Economy & Photovoltaics

CHRISTOPHER C. SWAN

Sierra Club Books   San Francisco

The Sierra Club, founded in 1892 by John Muir, has devoted itself to the study and protection of the earth's scenic and ecological resources—mountains, wetlands, woodlands, wild shores and rivers, deserts and plains. The publishing program of the Sierra Club offers books to the public as a nonprofit educational service in the hope that they may enlarge the public's understanding of the Club's basic concerns. The point of view expressed in each book, however, does not necessarily represent that of the Club. The Sierra Club has some sixty chapters coast to coast, in Canada, Hawaii, and Alaska. For information about how you may participate in its programs to preserve wilderness and the quality of life, please address inquiries to Sierra Club, 730 Polk Street, San Francisco, CA 94109.

**Library of Congress
Cataloging in Publication Data**

Swan, Christopher. *Suncell.*

Bibliography: p. 221. Includes index.
   1. Solar cells.
   2. Photovoltaic power generation.
TK2960.S93   1986   621.31′244   85–18394
ISBN 0–87156–751–2

Jacket design by Paul Bacon
Book design by Jon Goodchild
Illustrations by Christopher C. Swan
Printed in the United States of America
10 9 8 7 6 5 4 3 2 1

Contents

Suncell

SUNCELL

1: Source

Energy, Economy, and the Sun

E nergy is a primary force in all economies. The flow of energy
through an economic entity, whether a company, village, or
nation, organizes the economy. For more than fifteen years, the
industrialized nations of the world have been engaged in an
unprecedented dialogue concerning energy—where it is, how
much it costs, how we get it, and who owns it. Much of this dialogue, and the research work that has paralleled the talk, has
focused on discrete technical objectives. Relatively little concern
has surfaced around the social, political, and economic implications of specific technologies. Predictably, this apparent reticence
to discuss the more subjective values of technology is the result of
the often highly specialized perspective of the participants. Indeed,
for many decades the energy industry's specialists had barely been
heard from at all.

Moreover, the average person has generally been unconcerned
with the arcane subject of energy. But now the subject is out in the
open—and at a time when we are faced with unprecedented
choices that will profoundly influence both our economy and our
lives for many decades to come. Now, more than ever, it is critical
that we grasp as fully as possible the ramifications of various
energy technologies—socially, politically, and economically.

Until recently, discussion of energy technology centered around
nuclear power, coal, and alternatives within the general realm of
"solar energy." As late as 1980, photovoltaic cells were considered
to be a far-out technology that would not be commercially viable
until some time in the next century. Now, however, in discussions
about electrical-generation technology, nuclear power is no longer
considered an option and coal is seen as possible but not very
exciting. The big questions have become, How soon are photovoltaic cells going to become widely competitive? and How will the
spread of PV systems alter the entire business of generating
electricity?

In essence, photovoltaics, or "PVs," allow the direct transformation of incoming solar energy, light, into electricity. No fuel, no

moving parts, no smoke, no noise—and no necessary relationship between efficiency and scale—are involved. The event that permits this transformation occurs on an atomic scale within a thin wafer or coating.

Photovoltaic technology concerns light (photo) and electricity (voltaic). Just as fiber optic strands—now widely used to carry phone calls—composed of glass transmit information as pulses of light, so photovoltaics transform incoming pulses of sunlight, called photons, into electricity—that is, excited electrons. PV technology represents a quantum leap in simplifying the process of generating electricity. What has been considered a process that was most economical and technically feasible on a factory scale can now be done on the roofs of factories. Discussions of coal or nuclear power have always assumed that an enormous grid of high-voltage, neighborhood-scale electrical distribution systems was required. With PV technology, such systems would be unnecessary. What has been a service purchased by the month may soon become simply a consumer product to be purchased, like a new roof.

Photovoltaics present the possibility of a rapid transition to a solar economy with more than 80 percent of the existing buildings *in the world* becoming self-sufficient in electricity. Photovoltaics, in combination with a modicum of other renewable sources, may replace nearly all electrical generation by fossil or nuclear fuels within 35 to 50 years. They may also become a major source of energy for transportation as well. The implications of this technology for the United States and world economy are simply staggering.

The existence of PV technology, a worldwide industry devoted to photovoltaic cell production and development, effectively rewrites the criteria in electrical-generation technology. Decentralized, accessible, environmentally clean, inexhaustible, simple, and soon-to-be cheap electricity is possible. Indeed, it appears inevitable owing to the intrinsic simplicity of photovoltaics.

There is little doubt that the photovoltaic industry will become a billion dollar industry by 1990—multibillion by 2000—and it is inevitable, as with hundreds of previous waves of technological innovation, that this industry will have profound social effects. It will generate cultural and industrial opportunities, it will alter how we think about energy, and it may, within two decades, result in sweeping changes in the world's cultural and economic relationships. PVs represent an elemental change in the driving economic force of energy.

Earth's Energy Potential

Units of Measure

Tera = trillion
Terawatt = trillion watts
Terawatt hour = 1 trillion (1,000,000,000,000) watts in one hour
Energy consumption on Earth, annually = 50,000 terawatt hours, or
50,000,000,000,000,000 watt hours

The Energy We Receive Every Year, in Perpetuity

Direct Solar radiation	350,000,000 terawatt hours
Wind energy (potential)	200,000 terawatt hours
Sea thermal energy (potential)	100,000 terawatt hours
Wood waste energy (potential)	50,000 terawatt hours
Hydroelectric energy (potential)	30,000 terawatt hours
Geothermal energy (potential)	10,000 terawatt hours
Hydroelectric energy (developed)	3,000 terawatt hours
Tidal energy (potential)	1,000 terawatt hours
Total renewable	350,394,000 terawatt hours

The Energy Stored in the Earth (total potential supplies)

Coal	6,000,000 terawatt hours
Oil shale	1,500,000 terawatt hours
Uranium 235	1,500,000 terawatt hours
Petroleum	1,000,000 terawatt hours
Natural gas	400,000 terawatt hours
Tar sands	200,000 terawatt hours
Total nonrenewable	10,600,000 terawatt hours

The Total Energy Potential versus the Rate of Consumption

In twenty years, at our current rate of consumption (50,000 terawatt hours annually), we would consume about 9 percent of our total potential nonrenewable sources. Given our current dependence on petroleum, we could nearly exhaust this source within that time frame. Oil shale and tar sands represent a substantial potential, but like coal both entail serious environmental damage.

In 20 years, at current rates of consumption, if we consumed only renewable energy, we would consume about .00014 percent of the total energy income.

We *consume* nonrenewables; we *use* renewables.

(Source: Dasmann, Environmental Conservation)

Source

A wave travels across the sea. It is both an echo of force applied across the ocean's surface and a physical manifestation of unseen currents. To an observer on the edge of the sea, the ocean appears excited into a turbulent mass of interacting forces—wind, tide, and temperature.

Light traveling 93,000,000 miles from the ball of burning hydrogen called the sun passes into the sea to give its energy to molecules of hydrogen and oxygen—water. Photons from the sun excite electrons of the sea. Molecules heated by the sun rise toward the surface in upwelling currents, only to be cooled as their energy is transmitted by wind and evaporation across the ocean's surface. As if boiling at high temperature, the sea's top edge churns with currents, and life, that our eyes can barely see.

Manifestations are visible; the force is not. The single most pervasive form of energy we have known for millennia is light, yet only recently have we come to think of it as "energy." To call light energy is not merely an acknowledgment of the sun's life-giving power, and not just a statement of our knowledge of subatomic physics, but an affirmation of the sun's existence as the single source of energy and life.

We speak of wood, coal, oil, natural gas, even uranium, as if they were distinct from solar energy. We speak of solar energy as if it were a distinctly different form having no relation to fossil fuels. These are specious distinctions, dividing the subject of energy into different physical phenomena and masking the reality.

Fossil fuels are simply stored solar energy—wood relatively new and coal ancient. Wind, hydroelectric, and tidal energies are forces set in motion by the sun. We intercede with some device to capture and transmit the sun's energy. Using coal, oil, wood, and natural gas is like using up a solar battery. The Earth is a huge transformer and battery driven by the sun. Although the battery still contains a substantial charge, in the form of yet-to-be-exploited oil, natural gas, coal, and wood supplies, that charge has been depleted and what remains will not last. Coal supplies are estimated to be sufficient for more than a century, but at what cost to mine and burn? Oil supplies will clearly last through the remainder of this century and into the next, natural gas possibly longer, but how much more will it cost, in energy and money, to bring each successive well on-stream? And what will continued burning of oil and gas do to the atmosphere?

The most salient feature of solar energy used directly to heat or generate electricity is the simple fact that we can short circuit the entire complex process of developing, transporting, burning, and generating electricity with fossil fuels.

Pioneers who settled the inland valleys of the West in the nineteenth century perceived a lack of water. Above them, at the origins of rivers that flowed across their land, were deep forests and steep canyons. There they built dams, with highly elaborate pipelines and canals to bring the water to the farms down in the valleys. Only later did the farmers realize that beneath their feet

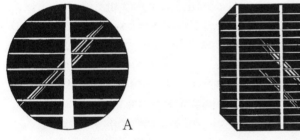

A

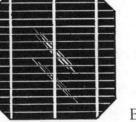

B

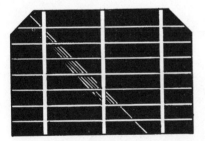

C

D

E

(a) The original round cell. Its shape results from the round ingot from which it is cut. Surface wires, or contacts, have been designed in numerous patterns. The structure of the contacts results from the need to reduce the distance electrons travel through the silicon to the contact while minimizing the blockage of valuable photons.

(b) Square cells with no corners, made by trimming a round cell. Single-crystal cells are now made by ARCO Solar this way in order to reduce the lost space between circles arranged in a module.

(c) Larger area square cells, made in a variety of rectangular shapes. Usually these are polycrystalline cells made by slicing a block of cast silicon into wafers.

(d) Ribbon cells are simpler to manufacture into modules than the other cells, since one need only slice a piece off with one simple cut. Mobil Solar has developed a technique for growing nine-sided ribbons.

(e) Amorphous cells, which can be virtually any shape. Amorphous is now produced in single small plates with steel or glass backing, or substrate, or in sheets produced from rolls of thin stainless steel. The surface contacts can be a matrix, a treelike shape, or a thin coating of tin oxide, conductive but transparent.

was a huge underground reservoir, thousands of feet deep and hundreds of miles in area, that the rivers they dammed had been regularly recharging for millennia.

Paralleling the development of modern agriculture we mined, logged, and drilled to secure ever larger sources of energy. Yet out in the plains of Texas there exists a double-walled adobe house, now only a shell devoid of roof or detail. The house had obviously been built by people who understood how to use natural forces to heat and cool a house. It was built in the mid-nineteenth century. A few people knew that much of the mining, logging, and drilling might have been unnecessary.

The development of a technology to transform solar energy directly is as much the development of a way of seeing as of using physical objects. Paradoxically, we had to go through all the steps of evolving heavy technology, from 1800 to 1970, to see that the source of energy was right in front of us and the technology to transform it directly was already in our possession. Like the farmers who could not see the water beneath their feet until they became so desperate that they drilled for it, we have seemingly had to exhaust all other fuels, all other possibilities, before seeing the source and the way to use it.

To understand solar energy one must attempt to perceive forces that are so subtle that they almost defy description. In picturing the workings of photovoltaic cells in the mind's eye, one is dealing

An illustration of the advantages of precisely square cells. All four panels can be made from essentially the same small square cell. Since the cells tend to be thinner than single-crystal cells, the resulting module is lighter and can therefore be larger. The large panel at bottom can be used to roof a building.

(Source: Mobil Solar Energy Corporation)

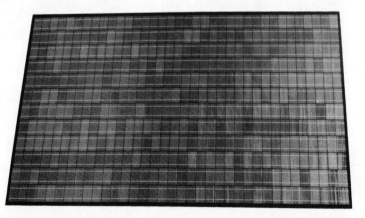

with the mechanics of light itself, on a level of perception where there is no light, only energy. It is as if the Earth resided in the midst of a constant wind of enormous power—yet so widely dispersed and pervasive that its effect upon us was both subtle and profound.

The sun gives us 178 trillion kilowatts of energy. A third of this solar wind bounces off our atmosphere, half heats the atmosphere, and a quarter evaporates water and creates clouds. Less than one-hundredth of the total causes photosynthesis to occur in plants, and less than a five-hundredth heats all our buildings and structures. We, and our buildings, are already solar heated regard-

Essential photovoltaics. The pressure of contained electrons bombarded by photons within the top layer of the cell causes electron flow through fingerlike wires laid atop the cell, through the circuit, through whatever is on that circuit, through a lightbulb, and back to the lower layer and equilibrium. It all happens because the electrons must seek a balanced state within the orbits of nuclei.

less of whether we advocate solar energy or not. Without sun, Earth dies.

We see the waves upon the sea, trees bending in the wind, rocks worn over centuries by wind-blown sand, and flowers bent low by a deluge of raindrops. The movement is transitory, but the pattern left behind is abiding testimony to the sun's power. Unlike more substantial machines, photovoltaics express, in elegant form, a transitory event that is like the single leaf bending in a breeze, minor by itself but major when the wind fills the forest.

Photovoltaics: What Are They?

Most photovoltaic cells are wafer-thin objects between 2 and 5 inches across, usually made of silicon and thin wire, that will generate electricity when placed in the sun. Photovoltaics were originally developed for consumer products by RCA in the late 1950s, but owing to lack of interest the solar-powered televisions and radios the company marketed did not sell. Photovoltaics came to the fore in the mid-1960s when NASA needed lightweight, relatively low power, but long-term sources of electricity to operate satellites—extension cords were out of the question.

Following the energy crisis of 1973–74, PVs began to attract attention as a serious source of electricity right here on Earth. Now, photovoltaic cells are the subject of intense research efforts by many governments and more than thirty corporations—sixteen corporations are now producing photovoltaics in the United States. An industry is seen on the horizon by hundreds of entrepreneurs, corporate managers, and scientists committed to all facets of photovoltaic development and marketing.

In the early 1970s photovoltaic companies devoted solely to

ARCO Solar's M-63 photovoltaic module. It has become a standard in the industry. Your basic, simple, elegant, dependable, medium-priced, durable, and adaptable Chevy of PVs.

(Source: ARCO Solar)

photovoltaic production were nonexistent, and the sales volume of the few companies that made photovoltaics was practically insignificant. In 1983 worldwide sales exceeded $250 million, and between 1981 and 1984 photovoltaic production quadrupled. In 1977 all photovoltaic manufacturers together produced sufficient photovoltaic cells to generate 500 kilowatts—500,000 watts, enough to light 5000 100-watt lightbulbs. In 1982 the worldwide photovoltaic industry produced 9.3 megawatts—9.3 million watts, enough to light 93,000 100-watt bulbs. In 1983 the industry produced 21.7 megawatts, enough to light 217,000 100-watt lightbulbs. Among industry analysts who watch the utility, oil, and general energy picture, there is widespread agreement that photovoltaics will become a major new industry with multibillion dollar potential in the early 1990s and probably a major energy source by the turn of the century—fifteen years from now.

The beginning of the photovoltaic industry could be roughly dated at 1975, when Solar Technology International was founded and Exxon purchased another pioneering company called Solar Power Corporation. Since then, and with most activity occurring in the 1979–84 period, the industry has seen a veritable explosion of research and development work into a boggling array of photovoltaic-cell technologies, both privately and publicly funded. It has further seen the development of more than 4000 photovoltaic installations on homes and hundreds of small remote-site facilities for everything from water pumping to microwave repeating. And it has seen three major 1-megawatt utility-scale photovoltaic facilities built within a few years with reliability exceeding 90 percent. Finally, a steadily growing number of private homes and commercial structures are now partially or wholly powered by the sun.

There is now no doubt that photovoltaics present the possibility of worldwide electrical generation that creates no noise, no air pollution, no international dependence, and no radioactivity. Within fifty years this technology may permit the total elimination of all fossil-fuel use—including mines, oil fields, distribution systems, power plants, electric grids, refineries, tankers, smog—and all nuclear-power use, although the sites and spent fuel will remain a problem.

Furthermore, photovoltaics present possibilities for cultural as well as technological change. Photovoltaics operate in ways, and on levels of energy, that are more akin to the life of a tree than to its end as wood in a furnace. And just as in some ways they mimic the order and intensity of biological forms around them, so photovoltaics can fit seamlessly into human organizations in all their myriad forms. Photovoltaics are inherently modular and endlessly expandable, they can be as efficient on your thumbnail as on the scale of a city block, and they can be assembled into all manner of systems, in any circumstances, and on practically any scale almost anywhere on the planet.

Photovoltaics seem to be a miraculous invention. Indeed, they appear to be so singularly amazing that we might be tempted to imagine the specter of some dark secret, some horrible vision of manufacturing madness, looming in the wings to wreak havoc. We have heard the story before, most recently as the proud boast of the budding nuclear industry of 1954. Nuclear energy would be so cheap, the claim went, that it would not need to be metered. Is there a dark side to the apparent wonder of photovoltaics akin to that of the nuclear story? The only serious drawback to PV technology is the toxic chemicals used in producing pure silicon for photovoltaics, but so far this appears to be a minor problem easily

An excellent example of how photovoltaics can be tastefully integrated into a building's design. The six Mobil Solar panels appear at first to be skylights but in fact are the home's source of electricity. This structure is on Block Island in Rhode Island.

(Source: Mobil Solar Energy Corporation)

solved. The entire process of producing photovoltaics, with the exception of the making of pure silicon, involves no particularly exotic or unusual technology or processes entailing serious environmental and safety problems. With the exception of silicon purification, all production steps are relatively simple and are as efficiently done on a small scale as a large one. Are photovoltaics a benign technology with no negative environmental impacts? It appears they are. PV technology in widespread use will not affect the air, temperature, noise level, vibration level, smell, species, or water of life.

The Conduct of Electrons

We can see emotion expressed in one another's faces but we cannot see the buzzing electrical energies within our brains that cause the muscles to reflect the emotions. We can see a flash of lightning but we cannot see the slow build-up of electrons that precedes it. We can feel the static electricity created by moving a balloon over the hairs on our arms but we cannot see the electrons dancing about.

Electricity is the excitation of electrons. All the electrical machinery we use in daily life is concerned with exciting electrons or subduing excited electrons. Electrical science is a body of knowledge almost entirely concerned with how to control and modulate the flow of excited electrons. Electricity is a noun, but it would be a verb if lexicographers were Einsteinians, because it is not a thing but an active event. Electricity is the phenomenon of excited electrons passing their charges, like relay runners passing on batons to the other runners.

In the language of electrical science, four key words are used to describe the event of electricity: *volt, ohm, amp,* and *watt.* The number of volts, or the voltage, is a measure of the force pushing electrical current. Amperage, or amps, is a measure of the volume of electrical current passing a given point within a specific time period. An ohm is a unit of measure describing the resistance to electrical flow inherent in any conductive material. Watts, or wattage, is a measure of work done in a unit of time. All four basic measures can be used to describe an electrical circuit's performance.

In an electrical circuit, there must be a completion to provide a circular route for electrical current. In the circuit are various devices that create resistance—lights, toasters—or electric motors that transform the excited electrons into other forms of energy. These forms might be more photons, as in a lightbulb, or mechanical energy, as in a motor's shaft. A lightbulb filament, for example, is composed of a material that can withstand high levels of heat and can be sufficiently resistant to glow white hot. Since the bulb is a nearly complete vacuum, no oxygen is present to allow the filament to burn, so what is given off are photons—light. Light-bulbs and any other devices placed on a circuit draw some of the energy off the circuit by transforming it into heat, light, or mechanical energy.

Our home appliances, streetlights, factory machines, and trolley cars are all on endless loops of electrical current energized by centralized power plants. These plants receive their energy from diverse sources—coal, oil, natural gas, uranium, or on-going flows of wind, water, and geothermal steam.

The Merging of Energy and Matter

Newtonian physics concerns the outward behavior of things in the world, things that are visible and moving. Einsteinian physics concerns the behavior of energy in space and time on levels barely seen and within events only briefly noted.

In the late eighteenth century, James Watt constructed the first steam engine. Its physical form and mechanical logic was a direct result of physical principles noted by Galileo, Newton, and many other scientists. All these men attempted to glean from certain events in the world around them a series of related natural laws. In our age, given our everyday use of elementary mechanics in everything from refrigerators to cars, observations such as "action generates reaction" may seem simple. But it was only the noting and mathematically quantifying of complex and subtle events in the physical world that yielded our very precise sense of just how these events could be duplicated in machines.

Hydroelectric generators and oil-fired electrical generating stations are the direct descendents of Watt's steam engine. Since the first large generating stations were built in the late nineteenth century, there have been countless refinements in the technology and its construction. As the mathematically described perception of mechanical events became more sophisticated, so did the machines of electricity. For example, in 1900 a crude casting process yielded workable castings for a generator frame. Forty years later, the same generator provided the electricity for a new casting process that yielded vastly improved generator casings. Developments leapfrogged, causing a co-evolutionary pattern, with one improvement begetting another over a period of decades.

As each subsequent innovation came into use, the drive for greater technological and economic efficiency caused designers to develop not only better machines but a wider variety of concepts and techniques related to the fundamentals of matter and electricity. Indeed, we began to study the phenomenon of electricity itself as well as the chemical and metallurgical qualities that affected its occurrence. This questioning, and the technology that resulted, is somehow capped by one of the most amazing technological ironies of our time—the creation of enormous and extraordinarily complex machines, with names such as cyclotron, to study nuclear phenomena. We have used, and still use, machines of gargantuan size and complexity to study the movement of particles so small they are invisible.

Albert Einstein, both in his work in the early 1900s on the photoelectric effect and the later work that led to his general theory of relativity, stated his observations and in the process rephrased a basic question: what is all this made of and why is it doing what it appears to be doing? This elemental question, coupled with Einstein's two primary theories, the photoelectric effect and relativity, formed the basis of modern physics. Further, it set the stage for a sequence of particle accelerators and related devices designed to explore the realm of atomic structure and the meaning of Einstein's theories. It is a curious irony that Einstein's work led to the development of nuclear power, both in power plants and weapons, as well as to the development of photovoltaic cells, for the former is associated with massive centralized power, both political and electrical, and the latter with decentralized power, political and electrical.

Perhaps the real irony of Einstein's work is the paradoxical turn of events that has occurred over the past eighty years. Massive technology born of Newton's universe was needed to build tools to study the atomic structure of Einstein's universe. In creating that technology, we are developing a way of seeing, and thus more new technologies that promise to eliminate categorically much of the technology that we used to get this far. Perhaps more than any other single development, photovoltaics characterize this shift in perception and technology.

Photons are pulses of energy streaming out in waves from the hydrogen fire known as the sun. A minute quantity of photons, about 178 trillion kilowatts, strikes the Earth; an even more minute quantity strikes the surface of existing photovoltaic cells; an even more minute quantity passes through the cells' crystalline lattice of atoms, which is surrounded by shells, or orbits, of electrons; and of those photons fewer still strike electrons and knock them out of their orbits to generate electrical current. The nucleus of each atom is in turn composed of many particles with vast spaces between them. The "matter" of it all is only perceivable on the scale at which we live. On the atomic level within a photovoltaic cell there is no matter, only energy.

The dance of protons and neutrons within the nucleus of an atom is echoed by orbiting particles we have only begun to name and that we can only observe by the tracks they leave behind in "bubble chambers." Circular or linear particle accelerators are like magnetic racetracks designed to push particles to speeds close to that of light and cause them to crash head-on into other particles. The resulting collisions cause particles to explode into a supercold chamber of liquid, where their momentary passage is recorded as a string of tiny bubbles.

Surrounding the dance of protons and neutrons within the nucleus are electrons traveling within shells, or orbits, around the nucleus. Waves of photons pass through this lattice of atoms like billions of asteroids passing through our solar system.

The "event" of photovoltaic electricity challenges us to leap from Newtonian to Einsteinian physics, from our daily perception of simple mechanics to a far more subtle conception of all that we see as energy in various states of being. Just as we have tended to perceive ourselves as apart and purely distinct from the sea only to find that we are almost entirely made of water and thus resonate with other "bodies" of water, so we have tended to perceive ourselves as distinct from the energies of life around us. But we are not apart. We are, inclusive of all our technology, as much an integral part of the energy continuum that is the universe as we are of the sea. Our development of semiconductors, photovoltaics, and the circuitry of microelectronics involves the perception and manipulation of electrical currents that are as subtle and seemingly insignificant as the currents within our brains. Increasingly, our highest technological efforts are focused on energy levels approximately equal to the energy in the nerves of a thumb.

Einstein saw as an ecologist sees. He perceived relationships in time and space as important, not merely as single events that could be isolated from their contexts. In physics, as in ecological science, we find ourselves facing the often chaotic and unpredictable implication that we cannot simply perform a single action, that everything we do has unanticipated consequences, and that furthermore the very act of observing an event can alter it.

Perhaps more than any other modern issue, the matter of energy has been subject to our most elemental perceptions. This is particularly important given the fact that we now live, and will for perhaps another decade or so, within a culture that is divided in its perception of energy. Many of us still habitually believe that only Newtonian principles as expressed in large, visible, and mechanical power plants will yield the appropriate energies necessary to drive our civilization. Simultaneously, a growing percentage of the population is gradually integrating Einsteinian thinking to the point where they no longer perceive energy as a "thing" that must be manufactured in large machines and in vast quantities. Paralleling these two ways of seeing are two subthemes: those who place value on the large machines of centralized power generation *tend* to perceive the flow of energy as dispersed from a centralized source, analogous to centralized political energy flowing outwards from the center; those who perceive energy as a phenomenon inextricably bound up in life itself *tend* to perceive the flow of energy as inherently dispersed and decentralized. Regardless of where one stands on these two ways of perceiving, it remains of critical importance, if we are to honestly address the problems we face as a civilization, that we become more precise and clear about our definition of energy.

The single most potent and portentous fact concerning photovoltaic cells demands that we alter our perception of what energy is. Photovoltaics are receptive to the level of the energy that we receive every day and that is already the prime mover of our planet, and this energy is streaming out from a nuclear-fusion generator so large its flares reach millions of miles and its fuel will burn for billions of years.

Manufacturing Power

In a firehouse in a small rural California town, a lightbulb was recently replaced. This bulb had been in its socket, burning every day, for almost 40 years. Its pure white light had glowed almost since the invention of the lightbulb as a store-bought product in the early 1900s. Early lightbulbs had implications of miraculous proportions and nearly sacred overtones. Suddenly we were free of darkness to an extent that was previously unimaginable and this would change our lives in uncountable ways. Making light, even if only a fire in a cave, has always been an act of considerable power. The fire, for millennia, has always been the light and the center of our circle in the night. Now the white light in its glass globe is so commonplace we forget how amazing it is. There ought to be a shrine to the lightbulb and its inventors.

City streets in the 1880s were often quagmires of mud in the winter and dusty plains dotted with horse excrement in the summer. In such a context, the apparently simple electric trolley, invented in the 1880s, was heralded as an achievement of technical wizardry—rapid transit—that would go far towards civilizing the urban environment. Electricity was seen as the agent of urban transportation change, and the light it later provided radically changed social habits. By the turn of the century, electricity was also becoming common in many factories, allowing the development of well-lit and electrically powered work stations.

We saw the lights, the wires above the trolley, and mentally linked the phenomenon of electricity to centralized power plants on the fringe of the city. This inextricable connection, whether we were conscious of it or not, led to the belief that electricity required some form of big "factory" to make it. This belief coincided with our increasing knowledge about how to generate electricity. By the 1920s the electrical networks, or grids, had spread throughout most of urbanized America, and engineers were realizing the economic advantages of vast centralized facilities—dams or fossil-fuel plants with generators as big as houses. Large factories required massive resource-acquisition schemes to secure sufficient raw materials. Coal mines dominated Appalachia in the 1920s and thirties, and in northern Pennsylvania and way out west in Los Angeles oil fields covered the hills. Most people who had electricity in the 1920s and thirties probably had some sense of where it came from and how it was generated, but there was little awareness of the implications of environmental degradation caused by the process. Today it appears that awareness has reversed; many seem highly aware of the environmental problems while relatively few have any idea where their electricity comes from or how it is generated.

It is often said that our civilization's morality lags behind its technological achievements. It is perhaps more true that our sense of what technology is necessary, and what institutions need to exist to maintain it, lag behind what is actually possible. While most remain unquestionably convinced that electricity must be generated, or manufactured, in large centralized facilities, it is becoming increasingly obvious to a small but growing portion of the population that photovoltaics and related solar technology open the door to a wholly new sequence of technologies and institutions that have the potential to alter our entire society.

The first rush of innovations in a new industry can result in an aura of wisdom and nearly invulnerable power that transcends short-term problems and propels the industry, its entrepreneurs, and its products into the future with a righteousness that remains overwhelming for decades. The electronics industry has just passed through a major wave of innovations, and the industry's aura has embraced countless publications. The individuals who have been affected are like converts to a new religion. Photovoltaics are now entering just such a period of intense innovation. The electrical-generation industry that we know today was born in such a period, between 1875 and 1900, and it appears likely that the photovoltaic industry will repeat that period almost exactly one century later.

In the late nineteenth century, the inventive geniuses of the period—Thomas Edison, Alexander Graham Bell, Charles Steinmetz, and Nicholai Tesla—were intensely interested in electrical phenomena. In much the same way as Silicon Valley entrepreneurs invented devices for computers in 1975, innovators in 1875 invented machines, appliances, and whole systems. They hovered between science fiction and science fact, between random dreams and solid laboratory experimentation. Generators, transformers, insulators, switches, motors, high-tension wires, and rectifiers—in short, the technology of electrical generation—were almost all invented between 1875 and 1900. And by 1920 the entire structure and subsequent form of utility companies had been defined; they only had to duplicate and expand themselves, fueled by the impetus of one period of innovation. Since then, countless entrepreneurs and technicians have created innumerable inventions that have improved the basic system, but few have had any impact on changing the form of that system.

We are now at a historical confluence between the past and a potential future, between an old way that began in a rush of wondrous invention more than a century ago and a new way that is just beginning to be felt. Obviously, we are witnessing the ending of one age and the beginning of another. To perceive just how profound a change photovoltaics could make over the next three to five decades, consider the changes wrought by the age now passing, and the righteous, secular attitude that often accompanied every new step. Each new generation of technicians raised under the guidelines, if not the spell, of Edison and Einstein developed ever more elegant, economical, and often beautiful machines of electrical power. Indeed, the power of these machines, and their creators, resulted in the definition of an industrial aesthetic. Electrical generation was, and remains, an art of economy, symmetry, and power.

To fully grasp the power of the age that began in the last quarter of the nineteenth century, the formative influence that technology had on our cities, and the implications of the new age and its technology, particularly photovoltaics, consider Los Angeles. This city is now electrified by what is perhaps the largest representative sample of the electricity-generating technology in use in the entire world.

Los Angeles is so big it is difficult to define as a city except on a map. Californians generally refer to the LA region as Southern California, by which they mean the vast urbanized landscape between Santa Barbara on the north and San Diego on the south. Although Los Angeles sits in the middle of this megalopolis, it is hardly distinguishable from the rest.

If one stares at a Federal Power Commission map of electric transmission lines in the western states, it soon becomes obvious who buys the lion's share of power—all the lines seem to point to

Southern California, and especially to the city of Los Angeles. Some of the lines extend north- and eastward for hundreds of miles. Their length and numbers only hint at the complex economic and political power games that once centered on power generation for the city, and that resulted in countless expansions of Los Angeles and its influence.

In the Sierra Nevada, more than 200 miles north of downtown Los Angeles, is a dam that was the city's first major hydroelectric project in the 1920s. Together, the dam and powerhouse were such a large construction project that the city built a railroad just to serve it. Massive turbines were set into tunnels blasted out of solid rock. Each tunnel was lined with concrete to make its walls smooth and precisely curved, like the inside of a snail's shell. Into each tunnel, which echoed in form the vortex of water that would soon flow through it, was placed an impellor the size of a ship's propellor (an *im*pellor is driven by a flow of water, a *pro*pellor pushes a ship through water).

When the plant was operational, the vanes of the impellors were struck by thousands of tons of cascading water contained within huge pipes. The impellors, spinning within the rush of water, turned tall shafts extending upward through the rock to a generator standing within a power plant.

Utility service areas in southern California: the coverage of Pacific Gas & Electric to the north and San Diego Gas & Electric to the south, with Los Angeles roughly outlined by a 150-mile circle. The lined area is the coverage of Southern California Edison Company. The white areas at right are primarily desert, very lightly populated. Within the urban region (defined by the circle) is a single large white area—a steep mountain range. In the eastern United States, the distribution pattern would be more evenly spread, reflecting the population distribution, but in much of the country there are large areas with no grid connections.

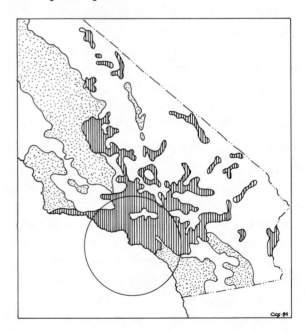

In essence, a generator is nothing more than two sets of magnets set in circles. One set is stationary, fixed to the generator case, and the second set is within the first and affixed to the impellor shaft. Each set of magnets has north and south poles, and a magnetic field extending outwards from each pole. As the rotating set of magnets spins within the containing fixed set, the poles constantly interact—positive, negative, positive, negative, positive, negative. This interaction of magnetic fields causes electrons to become excited within the magnetic structure.

The basic principle of an electrical generator is the same today as it was in the 1920s. While the city continues to use hydroelectric power, most of its electricity comes from other sources, primarily steam-generating stations fired by oil, natural gas, and nuclear fuel. In addition, Los Angeles purchases some power from coal-burning steam-generating stations in Arizona, but owing to the stringent antipollution measures common throughout Southern California, the city does not operate its own coal-burning facilities.

One hundred yards from the ocean beach, ten stories tall, a city block square, and surrounded by pumping oil wells, the Huntington Beach steam-generating station is an imposing machine. In essence the station is nothing more than a huge, very sophisticated

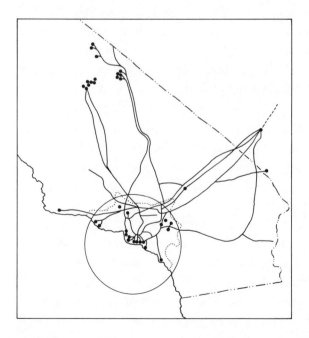

Sources of Southern California Edison's electricity. The dots represent major generating stations, the lines are high-voltage transmission lines. All the dots at top and on the far right are hydroelectric facilities located in the Sierra Nevada range and along the Colorado River. Within the circle defining the city of Los Angeles, practically all the plants are oil or natural-gas-fired steam-generating stations, with the major concentration along the city's waterfront area from Long Beach to Manhattan Beach. The dot on the coast farthest south is a nuclear power plant. SCE's major solar-thermal and photovoltaic plants are all on the circle's eastern periphery, at the edge of the desert.

teakettle. Oil or natural gas is burned in a large firebox to heat water until super-heated dry steam is generated. The steam is piped to large steam turbines, which are somewhat analogous, in performance if not shape, to the impellor in the hydroelectric system. Within the turbines' long round casing is a series of wheels on a shaft, each wheel composed of hundreds of small vanes. Steam under pressure is aimed through small nozzles at the vanes, causing the wheels to turn at high speed. The shafts of the turbines are connected to large generators.

Farther south on the ocean's edge stands the San Onofre nuclear power plant. Instead of oil, natural gas, or coal being burned in a boiler, here enriched uranium is "burned" within a heavily shielded reactor vessel, a very sophisticated bottle of water. This vessel contains the reaction, and its water is used to transfer heat to another, nonradioactive, water system. The latter is a fully enclosed system that generates steam used to drive turbines.

In addition to these primary hydroelectric and steam-generating sources, a number of smaller, less conventional sources also electrify the Los Angeles region. For example, various commercial buildings, with the assistance of the utility company, have developed on-site cogeneration facilities: they both produce electricity and use the waste heat produced by the gas turbines or diesel engines driving generators to heat water used in industrial processes. And out in the desert east of Los Angeles, geothermal power plants tap deep pockets of venting steam from the Earth's interior. The steam's heat is transferred to purer water, without corrosive salts, and the resulting steam is used to drive turbines.

Northeast of Los Angeles, near the city of Barstow, stands one of the most remarkable and beautiful power plants ever built. It is called "Solar One" and is the world's first large-scale solar-thermal generator. A field of large mirrors surrounds a tower with a ceramic casing at the top filled with circulating fluid. As the sun rises, the mirrors begin tracking its movement, focusing its light on the tower's ceramic top until that top turns white hot. The circulating fluid carries the heat down the tower and through a sequence of heat exchangers that generate steam. The steam is piped to turbines that drive generators.

Due east of downtown Los Angeles, on a high plain near San Bernardino, is a photovoltaic power plant that tracks the sun much as the Solar One plant's mirrors follow the sun. However, rather

than focusing the light on a central tower, the photovoltaics simply
track the sun and convert its light directly into electricity. Finally,
scattered around the Los Angeles basin are clusters of windmills,
each generating electricity directly from the wind.

The assemblage of machines powering Los Angeles, built over
decades and involving billions of dollars in invested capital, represents both the culmination of an entrepreneurial dream that began
more than eighty years ago and the beginning of a new entrepreneurial dream that has profound implications. It also represents a
considerable degree of technological ability and unparalleled agreement on the how and why of electrical generation. But perhaps
more than anything else the system represents a commitment to the
idea that electricity has to be manufactured somewhere.

Los Angeles has one brilliant asset, plenty of sun, and one dim
liability, plenty of dirty air. The city's primary utility, Southern
California Edison, has already shifted towards an aggressive policy
of developing renewable energy sources, particularly photovoltaics. The city's air pollution is caused more by automobiles than by
oil-burning or natural-gas-burning steam-generating stations. Los
Angeles once supported a 1200-mile interurban rail system, in the
1920s probably the largest in the world, which was abandoned in
favor of more cars and freeways between 1940 and 1960. This shift
was the result of a carefully planned strategy by General Motors
and other major auto-industry corporations, who later profited by
the sale of more cars and buses. Now the city is beginning construction of a new light-rail trolley. Ironically, the system will be
built on the route of the last remnant of the original electric rail-
way. The city is also sponsoring one of the most aggressive and
well-managed energy-conservation strategies in the United States.
Clearly, Los Angeles exists within a context for change.

Photovoltaic cells, in combination with existing storage systems, could be used to electrify practically the entire city of Los
Angeles—residences, commercial structures, and all forms of
transportation. Used in combination with solar heating and cooling
systems, windmills atop buildings near the beach and on the mountain ridges that rim the city, and small-scale hydroelectric facilities,
photovoltaics could be the dominant means of supplying the city
with energy.

Within fifty years—twenty-five if the transition became a
"crash program"—Los Angeles and its environs could be totally

reliant upon solar and renewable sources of energy. Air pollution could be practically eliminated, and one would be able to stand on a streetcorner and see the snow-covered mountains to the east, a rare sight in the Los Angeles of the 1980s. Property values could well rise along with trees, which would grow more rapidly and remain healthier under the clear skies. With its already incredible diversity of culture, Los Angeles would rise in value immeasurably.

A New Look at Efficiency

Efficiency is a peculiar word in the lexicon of technology. *Efficiency* is used to describe an objective measurement, but it is also used to describe a subjective quality of a specific machine or technological system. Thus, a utility engineer might call a steam turbine 80 percent efficient, meaning that only 80 percent of the steam entering the turbine is transformed into mechanical energy, with 20 percent lost as friction in the bearings and heat escaping through the turbine casing. In contrast, a financial planner for the utility industry might describe a particular process of generating electricity—including the financial aspects—as efficient. Typically this might mean its operating costs are low, or its labor costs are minimal. The engineer would be using the term to describe a measurable effect while the financial planner might be stating a subjective belief, based on hard technical data *and* an intuitive perception of the system's economics.

How the term *efficient* is used can reveal both the bias of the speaker and the diversity of views possible with respect to a specific technological system. An engineer extolling the efficiency of a steam turbine, for example, might be highly specialized in the arcane world of steam-turbine design. As such, he or she might be far more interested in impressing colleagues with the efficiency of a particular design than with that of an entire utility system, of which the steam turbine would be only a part. The financial planner, on the other hand, might be nearly obsessed with the economics of a particular technology as revealed on a balance sheet but have little appreciation of the potential efficiencies of new technology or of the economic implications and inefficiencies of pollution. Both specialists might be right in their use of the word *efficient*, and both would certainly use the term correctly within the context of their respective professions. But neither would be able to identify the most efficient means of energizing a home.

Comparing renewables and nonrenewables complicates the definition of efficiency. A gallon of gasoline is effectively irreplaceable and thus limited by the volume that remains untapped within the Earth. As the available supply dwindles, or so the story goes, the price will go up. If we are even to minimize, not to mention eliminate, the impact of this rising cost, we must, quite simply, use less fuel. That is, we must use less and less gasoline within ever more efficient machines to accomplish what we do now. Obviously, efficiency is of paramount importance relative to dwindling supplies of fossil fuels.

By contrast, the energy potential of renewable sources is effectively inexhaustible. Wind, hydro, geothermal, wood, and biomass energies are limited by local conditions, but we are nowhere near exhausting those resources. And photovoltaics are practically unlimited in their potential energy output. For a sense of just how unlimited the potential is, consider: practically any house in the United States could be electrified with photovoltaics equal in area to 35 by 35 feet, and an electric car could be recharged as well were the area twice that size. Given this potential, and the renewable nature of all solar sources, efficiency becomes simply a measurement of the transformation process, with no necessary reference at all to scarcity of the source.

The concept of *net energy analysis* further complicates our understanding of *efficiency*. Net energy analysis results from the application of standard accounting procedures to the generation of energy. Basic to corporate accounting are various techniques for assessing the return on a specific investment. Typically, a major improvement is analyzed to ensure that its cost is returned by the savings it allows in overall efficiency. If the improvement will not yield a sufficient return—that is, one covering more than its cost—then no profit, or net gain, will accrue from the improvement.

Applying net energy analysis to energy development and generating systems often causes a radical shift in how we view a particular technology. A typical nuclear power plant requires eight to twelve years to construct, and during that construction period a considerable amount of energy is consumed both by the plant's component manufacture and its on-site building. This energy might be equal to fifteen to eighteen years of the nuclear plant's potential output in electricity once it begins to operate. At best, the typical nuclear plant might last thirty to thirty-five years, although recent evidence suggests radioactive bombardment of reactor materials may weaken the structure and result in premature plant closing.

Further, during that lifetime the typical plant will actually operate at sufficient power to energize the grid only 50 percent of the time, though many nuclear power plants operate at full power considerably less than 50 percent of the time. Thus, the net energy gain—the profit—of such a plant may be only a dubious possibility. And of course a net energy analysis of nuclear power plants made now, in the 1980s, would not include the unknown, and probably quite substantial, energy costs of decommissioning nuclear power plants and disposing of their waste.

Owing in part to the environmental movement and resulting legislation requiring the assessment of environmental impacts, and owing to the technology and costs associated with environmental mitigation—such as installing stack scrubbers to diminish particulate pollution from a coal-burning power plant—we now have a body of knowledge regarding the health and environmental costs of technological processes. However, although the health effects of a specific technology may be well known, their real costs may be only partially reflected in a financial document. For example, safety equipment for coal-mine workers would be an accountable expense, while some forms of lung disease or arthritis might appear only indirectly as a hospitalization cost, not as a "life-shortened" cost. Similarly, the cost of a particular environmental problem, such as stack particulates, might show up on an expense sheet but the longer term, multibillion dollar cost of acid rain killing forests and agricultural land would not appear on any single balance sheet. Such uncounted "expenses" usually end up, if they are not dismissed entirely, as taxpayer expenses to be covered through government programs.

Regardless of how we treat these costs, or of how subjective their valuation might be, practically all conventional forms of generating electricity have serious and potentially very expensive side effects that we can no longer ignore.

Inevitably, a thorough assessment of the full costs of all forms of electrical generation brings us to the realization that our dependence on conventional systems—oil, gas, coal, and nuclear facilities—requires that we accept these costs. We may be able to diminish the costs over time, but we will never be able to eliminate many of the side effects, for they are inherent in the technology. However, we can use the knowledge we have to develop criteria for new technologies that will replace the old. In the process, we can expand the definition of efficiency to embrace *all* facets of the process, not just the mechanical.

Until recently, the argument that a new technology had to be entirely, or almost entirely, nonpolluting was moot, since everyone assumed that any means of generating electricity would entail some adverse environmental side effects. Now the existence of solar buildings, hot-water systems, windmills, small hydro generators, solar-thermal, and various other renewable technologies, especially photovoltaics, sets a totally new standard. There is no doubt that these technologies can be developed to involve only a small fraction of the environmental and health problems that are associated with conventional technology. So it is now possible to assess all electrical-generation technology with respect to the broadest definition of efficiency, inclusive of all costs.

In the late 1960s and early 1970s, when photovoltaics were first introduced as a possibility, their efficiency was a subject of concern. Nine to thirteen percent of the light striking the cells is transformed into electricity, and most energy-industry people felt that this low efficiency rate would dramatically limit the market potential of photovoltaics. Inevitably, critics pointed to the high efficiency of coal-burning power stations, which convert more than 40 percent of their incoming energy into electricity, to prove the weakness of this new technological upstart.

But comparing photovoltaics and conventional electrical-generating systems involves fundamental problems in perception, as the following example shows. In the mid-seventies, various groups began promoting the idea of a space-power satellite. Essentially the concept involved the construction of a multiwinged PV-carrying satellite in space that would use microwaves to beam energy down to Earth. The concept was touted as a space-age solution that would dramatically increase PV efficiency and preserve the centralized plant and grid system, which the satellite would plug into. Technically, the concept is quite feasible. However, it would retain the vulnerability of centralized power plants to natural or human-made disruption, it would cost substantial amounts of highly expensive rocket fuel, it would require a series of rocket flights involving large sums of money, and it would commit us to a system "out there" that would always be difficult to repair or modify. Why do it? It would increase PV efficiency, but so what?

The concept of the space-power satellite evolved from an inherently incomplete perception of the "problem." The ultimate objective of this solution was to meet the technical and financial needs of centralized utility companies, regardless of whether these needs accurately reflected market needs. Furthermore, the concept did not even attempt to address, let alone solve, the various social and environmental problems linked to centralized electrical generation of *any* kind. Finally, the transmission of electrical energy by powerful microwaves through the living atmosphere may well be equivalent in environmental impact to pouring smoke into the sky.

If we turn our perception of the problem around, looking not at the efficiency and technical form of the utility enterprise but at its end uses, then we begin to redefine the problem totally. Looking at end uses in an electrical-generation system is analogous to making the first step in analyzing the feasibility of any technology—that is, conducting a market study.

A market study is not simply the compilation of a bunch of demographic numbers; it is a thorough analysis of who uses a product, how they use it, how much they use when they use it, and in what form they use it. The conclusions of such a study of electrical generation, based on extrapolations from information already generated by a variety of studies over the past decade, would point to the need of a relatively low level of electricity for household appliances and lights and a modest level of heat energy on many days of the year. With no sacrifice in living standards, most Americans could cut their energy consumption by 50 percent by conservation measures alone. By interpreting the rate of consumption in electricity and heat, and comparing that rate to the quantity of energy the average home receives from the sun, we soon discover that the problem is not one of importing energy from anywhere, but of using the energy the house receives anyway. The same would be true of most commercial and industrial facilities. In this context, even with photovoltaics capturing only 6 to 15 percent of the light the building receives, we discover that it is possible to cover practically any conceivable electrical need in homes and most in commercial facilities.

Furthermore, if we analyze the *entire* process of generating electricity with coal, oil, natural gas, or uranium from the standpoint of overall efficiency, the final output of energy, the end use, may itself represent no more than 15 to 20 percent of the fuel's

potential energy. Mining, drilling, processing, refining, transporting, generating, transmitting, and controlling use all require
energy. It is the delivered product, the amount of electricity entering a house, that is the critical efficiency figure.

Photovoltaics now on the market can consistently produce electricity at midday efficiencies of 9 to 13 percent. Photovoltaics in
the labs in 1984 are reaching 20 to 25 percent efficiencies, and
photovoltaics in the mind are theoretically capable of 30 to 40 percent efficiencies. Clearly, where the measure is end-use efficiency,
the technology is now competitive.

Energy Politics

E lectrical, water, transportation, and communication systems are the infrastructures upon which the entire culture, and all its commerce, rests. Characteristically, the companies and government agencies that manage our infrastructures tend to be cautious and conservative, understandable attitudes given the fact that most infrastructures involve massive maintenance expenditures and even larger expansion and modifying expenses. Utilities and railroads, as a matter of course, spend billions annually just to keep their physical plants in working order.

Reflecting the conservatism and solidity of the utility industry, its management has long been characterized as extraordinarily careful, particularly when it comes to developing new power plants. Utility-management people know all too well how expensive an error or policy shift can be on the multibillion dollar level, not merely in money, but in economic ripple effects where customers are affected. All of us, as utility customers, tend to perceive utilities as if they were all-pervasive agencies equal to government and sanctioned by the heavens. Since we pay so little attention to utilities, and since so few of us accurately perceive from their point of view the problems we all face, we tend to expect these organizations to act with uncommon sensibility and wisdom, even when the rest of the world seems to be going bananas.

Although some utilities are municipally owned, or, like the Tennessee Valley Authority, are regional entities with substantial ties to the federal government, most are private and profitable corporations whose form and service are precisely delineated by government regulation. As is the case with most infrastructures operated by private companies, utilities have been more closely regulated than other industries. Inevitably, regulation has led to the politicization of energy development and use. Congress and state legislatures, as well as local county and state bodies, can have considerable influence over utility-company policies and planning directions.

Gradually, over a period of decades, the utility industry and its counterparts within government regulatory agencies have come to agree on basic policy and long-term directions. Until the early 1970s, this was a relatively comfortable arrangement, with each party sharing the common view that large centralized power plants, increased consumption, and an expanded electrical grid were in the best interests of the entire society. The definition of what was effi-

The Energy We Use in the United States

Before the industrial revolution, a "primitive" individual might have consumed 15,000 kilocalories of energy per day in the form of food, cooking energy, and animal feed. Now the average American consumes 16 times more—250,000 kilocalories per day per person.

Americans consume energy at a prodigious rate.

For every 100 units of energy an American consumes
a resident of Great Britain consumes 48,
a resident of the U.S.S.R. consumes 46,
a resident of Japan consumes 33,
a resident of Mexico consumes 11,
a resident of China consumes 5,
a resident of India consumes 1.

Where does the energy Americans use come from?

In 1980, domestic petroleum and natural gas supplied 52 percent,
imported petroleum and natural gas supplied 22 percent,
coal supplied 19 percent,
nuclear fission supplied 3 percent,
hydroelectric, geothermal, and other supplied 4 percent.

Petroleum, which includes gasoline, kerosene, aviation fuel, heating oil, butane, propane, diesel fuel, and natural gas, supplied 74 percent of our needs.

What do we use the energy for?

In 1980, general manufacturing consumed 45 percent,
transportation consumed 22 percent,
household operation consumed 20 percent,
miscellaneous commercial consumption was 13 percent.

More than half of the 22 percent used for transportation went to automobiles, socially efficient tools that are grossly inefficient in energy terms. The real cost, that is all-inclusive, of operating an automobile may be at least 40 cents per mile and possibly as high as 60 cents per mile. *All* other forms of transportation using a fossil fuel cost in the range of 5 to 20 cents per mile.

Of the 20 percent consumed in household operation, more than half is consumed in heating only, and much of the remainder is consumed in lighting, which generates more heat than light due to the inefficiency of incandescent lightbulbs.

cient and what was not, the form of technology to be developed, and the principal players in the game of generating electricity were all agreed upon. Certainly, occasional spats or long-term struggles occurred between regulators and regulatees, but everyone remained reasonable and civil. Until the early 1970s.

Beginning in the late sixties, the environmental movement caused a sequence of increasingly stringent air- and water-pollution measures to be adopted on the state and federal level. Pollution that had been acceptable was increasingly being seen as a problem of very serious proportions. In response, the utility industry began designing and installing, at substantial cost, various forms of anti-pollution equipment. A few years later, when it seemed that nuclear power was finally going to take off as a major new industry, utilities began committing vast sums of money for new reactors. Then, just as they were recovering from the financial and organizational shock of air-pollution laws, the energy crisis hit. Overnight, everyone became obsessed with conservation, and a steadily growing portion of the population began to realize just how much of our energy resources we had been wasting. At the same time it became increasingly apparent to even the most conservative planners that, owing to a slowdown in population growth and to the effects of conservation, growth in electrical consumption would not be sustained. That realization undercut the demand for many new power plants. At the same time, the government was encouraging conservation and a policy of energy independence.

Meanwhile, back at the power plants, utilities were finding that the plethora of government regulations pertaining to equal opportunity hiring, occupational safety, and environmental impact—most passed in the late sixties and early seventies—were causing all sorts of management problems and delays in the construction of new plants. Simultaneously, the public was increasingly questioning the validity of utility claims that new power plants were even necessary. The results were lawsuits, legal delays, and sheer complexity in management and planning.

In the thick of this situation, the federal government began to encourage utilities to build coal-power plants, since we had plenty of domestic coal and the technology was, compared to nuclear, cheaper and more reliable. Thus, many utilities began to shift gears and go back to coal, either converting oil-burning plants to coal again or designing new coal-burning plants. This in turn raised a whole sequence of issues with environmentalists that resulted in more lawsuits and delays.

The climax was Three Mile Island, a near meltdown of a nuclear reactor in Pennsylvania that many industry observers now feel was the last nail in the coffin of nuclear power in the United States. To utilities, nuclear had been a bright hope in the early seventies, but by 1980 for most companies it was a moot point.

Given the longstanding and nearly legendary conservatism of the utility industry and its often exemplary management by the most pragmatic corporate managers in the world, the 1970s were years of profound change. An industry with carefully nurtured relationships in the business and political realms, an industry characterized by dependability and stability, suddenly found itself being flogged in the courts, berated by government officials one year and embraced the next, and courted by suppliers of technologies who went bankrupt, only to be replaced by new companies with no utility experience at all. As if that were not enough, the industry could not even depend upon its own growth projections. In short, the utility industry in the 1970s found it could not depend on *anything* except its own will to survive.

Without doubt, the single most profound change of the 1970s was the maturation of a wholly new constituency, dominated by the baby-boom generation. This generation's understanding of environmental and social issues resulted in a new agenda in the discussion of how energy was to be generated and utilized. As it evolved in political discussions of the early seventies, this agenda centered around the disturbing fact that the United States consumes a quarter to a third of the world's energy supply—from conventional sources—to support only 5 percent of the world's population. In the period in which the debate began, roughly between 1970 and 1974, it was still assumed that electrical consumption would rise on a per capita basis and that the nation's population would rise significantly by the year 2000. Based on such a forecast, the utility industry and federal government agencies like the Department of Energy were planning a massive expansion of conventional coal and nuclear power plants. The article of faith upon which the proposed expansion rested: growth equals more consumption and growth is good. Given this context, and the tendency for the new constituency to question not only the validity of the utility industry's forecasts but the very existence of a utility industry, the conflict between industry and its new critics centered, and centers, on very elementary issues.

This new constituency is aligned with environmental organizations, consumer groups, and the renewable-energy industry, in general philosophy if not on specific technologies. Overall, the views held by this group tend toward a generalist rather than specialist perspective. This constituency has taken the ecologist's precept, you cannot do just one thing, and begun exploring all of life from that point of view. Seeing energy use from that standpoint results in a radically different view of what is technically workable and efficient in the broadest sense. One begins to see energy as nearly all of life. Indeed, the word *energy* is commonly used in conversation to cover a multiplicity of actions and emotions. In many circles energy is recognized as an all-pervasive phenomenon in which we are inextricable players.

At this writing, in 1985, the distinctions between this new vision of energy, including the politics that evolve from it, and the more established views are less pronounced. The intensity of the debate has subsided somewhat as many former critics of the utility industry have themselves become involved in the utility, solar, and photovoltaic industries. Certainly the rapid development of renewable-energy technology, even by utilities, is testament to the value of the new vision—it is being accepted. But there remain strong arguments for coal, nuclear, and other large-scale technologies for electrical generation.

As if attempting to rewrite history, the Reagan administration remains committed to revitalizing the nuclear-power industry. It holds this policy despite the industry's widely publicized problems, and despite the fact that repeated polls have indicated that by a clear majority Americans favor solar-energy development. Even *Forbes,* a respected business magazine favorable to the Reagan administration, considers the U.S. nuclear industry a monumental managerial disaster—the worst ever, in fact. No utilities in the United States are even including nuclear power in their future planning. Yet the White House seems to be unaware of these facts. On the contrary, it appears to have a tacit policy, not fully articulated at the time of this writing, to accelerate licensing programs and otherwise assist the nuclear industry back to health.

It is an irony of the Reagan administration's policies that they purport to be "conservative" free-enterprise positions focused on what is perhaps the most non-entrepreneurial and heavily subsidized industry the world has ever seen. Nuclear power has never been a profitable business, and now we face the prospect of still more subsidies to dispose of nuclear waste and decommissioned power plants and thus to extricate the economy from the entire nuclear debacle. It is also curious that an administration so concerned with national security remains committed to extremely vulnerable centralized nuclear power plants. A relatively small group of terrorists could very rapidly take advantage of this vulnerability, with frightening consequences.

In the energy politics of 1985, nuclear energy is dormant, if not dead altogether. A major campaign emanating from the White House might result in a modest resurgence of the nuclear industry, but this is highly doubtful. The utilities appear to be in a philosophical department store: when in doubt entertain everything. With the exception of a few regional utilities that made it through the 1970s without a major financial or political problem, most utilities are exploring many options, including renewables of all kinds, and are taking a wait-and-see attitude. More coal-fired plants are being built, or are planned for construction in the 1990s, but there is no industrywide consensus that coal is *it*. Many utilities, notably those in the Northeast and air-pollution-prone Sunbelt cities, either cannot economically justify coal-burning plants or would face serious environmental problems in building them. Renewable energy, particularly photovoltaics, appears increasingly attractive, but for many in the utility business solar still raises a raft of technical and strategic questions, some threatening the very idea of a utility company.

The growth of a new and more critical constituency in the 1970s not only challenged the technological premises on which conventional electrical-generating systems were based, but it resulted in a deep re-examination of the social premises as well. Viewed in the light of social value, nuclear power is a highly sophisticated technology requiring a technocratic elite with nearly superhuman capabilities. The coal industry is, to a great extent, built upon the destruction of whole regions—reclamation is possible, is done, but the new land will never be the same—and the servitude of miners willing to risk their lives in dark tunnels. Both technologies involve the continuance of socially unhealthy and environmentally dangerous practices, risks taken at a time when it appears that environmental pollution, particularly acid rain and toxic waste in water supplies, is becoming more pervasive and insidious. Indeed, the distinction between environmental "impact" and social costs is diminishing.

In the terms of energy politics of the 1970s, photovoltaics rewrite the rules of the game, socially as well as environmentally. Photovoltaics, and to a lesser extent all renewable technology, present the possibility of radically decentralized means of electrical generation that is accessible, technically and economically, to a large percentage of the population. Regardless of who produces the photovoltaic modules, whether Japanese electronics companies or American oil companies, once the product is sold, it represents one more unit of electrical-generating capacity that is not being provided by a utility company's centralized conventional power plants. As photovoltaics become more widely known, available, and competitive, it will be possible for those who no longer wish to purchase utility power, for whatever reason, simply to cut the cord. The issue of which technological option to pursue is thus no longer a decision almost totally within the province of utilities and government; it is rapidly becoming a consumer decision.

The energy politics of the late 1980s are likely to be dominated by two apparently conflicting but possibly compatible strategies. Most utilities will either sit tight and wait, or they will continue to pursue a strategy of conservation, using small-scale fossil-fuel plants, and perhaps dabbling in renewables and various efficiency improvements with existing technology. They will buy time. This course represents a safe and literally conservative strategy. It is consistent with the fact that the United States could reduce its electrical consumption by 30 to 50 percent with no change in basic lifestyle. Although few utilities would openly state that such a reduction in consumption is a serious policy, many within the industry know we are, as a nation, comfortable in energy terms. A relative handful of utilities are moving in quite a different direction by developing a strategy that involves conservation, solarization, and the widest possible range of small-scale renewable sources, including photovoltaics. This second course is inherently fraught with greater risks, mainly financial, and a host of unknowns relative to the utility industry's form. Will the industry die as a result of new small-scale renewable technologies or will it embrace the new technologies and find a way to market them and

Renewable Energy Process

Large-scale hydroelectric

Need: One or two or three free-flowing rivers
Politics: Can we dam this river?
Construction: Move massive volumes of dirt and rock
Time: Five to fifteen years
Complexity: Potentially very complex
Money: $500 million to a few billion
Environment: Water table, species, and habitat change or destruction

Small-scale hydroelectric

Need: One free-flowing river or creek
Politics: Can we dam this creek?
Construction: A few basic machines and some shovels
Time: A few months to two years
Complexity: Low-technology, basic electricity
Money: $5000 to $5 million
Environment: Possibly major change in marine life, a slight hum

Wind

Need: Bare hilltop or open windy plain
Politics: Low impact, minimal objections if not too many windmills
Construction: One tractor, a pick-up truck, and hand tools
Time: A few weeks to install, a few months to assemble hardware
Complexity: Low-tech, basic electricity, manufactured components
Money: $5000 to $10 million
Environment: Visually ugly to some, a whirring noise when windy

Geothermal

Need: A site containing water and volcanic vents
Politics: Usually none unless facility is large
Construction: Complex heat-transfer and generation equipment
Time: Two to eight years
Complexity: Can be very complex and sophisticated
Money: From a few million to ?
Environment: Sometimes noisy, can release hot water into local waters

Photovoltaic

Need: A suitably sunny place—a roof, field, parking lot, etc.
Politics: Would anyone care?
Construction: Basic hand tools, possibly a small tractor or crane
Time: A few weeks to a year for a 1-megawatt or larger plant
Complexity: Many homeowners and practically all electricians could do it
Money: $500 to $5 million, depending on scale
Environment: No noise, no smoke, no change in plant or animal life

make a buck? This is an open question, and with every drop in photovoltaic prices the question looms larger.

The energy politics of the next ten years may be driven by the simple fact that renewable technologies, especially photovoltaics, are so technically simple that installation and operation do not require an elite corps of specialists. And since renewables can be decentralized to a degree unimaginable with any other technology, there need not be a regulatory body to oversee development, so development could become strictly a local issue. In short, PV and its companion renewable technologies are highly compatible with the American values of self-reliance and liberty, values that in this case need not be muted by fear of who has a hand on the light switch.

The basis of self-reliance is a sense of security that comes from mastering the elements of living. In the knowledge that you are capable of coping with a wide range of technological and social problems you become more solidly grounded in day-to-day realities. When the technology of life becomes so complex and specialized that it is divorced from everyday reality and isolated in an arcane profession, most of the population has increasing difficulty understanding the technology upon which it depends, let alone installing, repairing, buying, or selling it. As a consequence, self-reliance becomes a distant possibility seen through a fog of technical abstractions and dependencies on technologies and people one cannot know—the utility becomes "they."

The utility systems of the United States, and of most industrialized countries, are highly sophisticated systems operated by a relatively small social group that possesses specialized knowledge. Major institutions, oil companies, and government agencies concern themselves with securing our oil supplies. Their actions are abstract strategic moves almost entirely divorced from the daily realities of the vast majority. Predictably, just as a sense of personal self-reliance is lost in the complexity and distance of sophisticated institutions, so also is our sense of security lost in an indistinct realm of abstractions. Security itself becomes a business, not a state of mind. Police and military agencies become specialists in maintaining a state of security, the security of the state. Indeed, there is a close relationship between multinational oil companies engaged in exploration in politically unstable regions of the world, our dependency on oil, and our military "security" forces.

In an age of jet travel and instantaneous global communication, maintaining the integrity of national borders is practically impossible. A small army of terrorists could arrive in three-piece suits on the five o'clock flight from somewhere, convene in a conference room at a major hotel in the evening, and a week later complete the devastation of a few key utility facilities. The region's economy would be massively disrupted and the terrorists would be scattered over five cities before the security forces figured out who might have staged the attack. Given this context, the highly sophisticated weaponry of industrialized nations, especially nuclear weapons, is the modern equivalent of a Maginot Line—useless. Yet military planners go right on building ever more elaborate tools of "security" at great cost. Meanwhile, the real threat is free practically to walk across the border. Evidently military planners are still inventing weapons for the last war, as if international conflicts still occurred along neatly delineated borders.

It is difficult to imagine precisely how it would feel to live in an industrialized nation that was not so vulnerable, that was reliant upon a diversity of locally based renewable energy sources. It is conceivable that the full development of renewables, especially PVs, would result in a gradual lessening of international tensions. The value of Mideast oil would diminish, as would the necessity of maintaining a military presence in the region. The vulnerability of centralized power plants, along with their use, would diminish. In time there would be an increase in the individual's sense of real security. With PVs on the roof, or nearby, and a smattering of other electrical sources plus an electric car recharged by PVs, each neighborhood, and in many cases each house, would be a self-reliant entity insofar as energy was concerned. Beyond the decline in world military presence, how would such a development change our perception of security?

Earthquakes, floods, tornadoes, windstorms, lightning, hurricanes, landslides, and blizzards commonly wreak havoc upon relatively delicate infrastructures. To the extent that renewable and home- or neighborhood-based power systems were in place, the trauma of such events would be minimized. Whether the destruction was due to natural events or human conflict, it would be possible to quickly re-establish electricity and all the services it powers—particularly medical. Regional blackouts lasting for days, even weeks, would be replaced by power outages in single struc-

tures or perhaps neighborhoods lasting no more than hours. And in
many cases the necessary repair work would be accomplished by
local residents, not specialists whose availability was tightly limited. In the broad overview, then, the development of photovoltaics
presents the possibility of a more self-reliant and secure society
that relies on the power of its entire populace, not on the chimeri-
cal nature of abstract institutions.

SUNCELL

2: PV Business

The Invisible Action of Photovoltaic Cells

A photovoltaic cell is a semiconductor device that is capable of transforming light energy, photons, into electrical energy, electrons. Photovoltaics can be made with many materials and combinations of materials but most, in current production, are made of silicon. Silicon cells are made as wafers cut from round ingots, as ribbons "grown" from a bath of molten silicon, or as a very thin coating laid upon another material like printing ink on paper.

PVs operate by what is called the photoelectrical effect. The bombardment of atoms by light, photon particles, can cause electrons within certain substances to become excited and alter their positions. If a conductive element is close by, and if the substance being bombarded by photons is so composed that it contains an internal imbalance in its atomic structure, and if the conductive element, usually a wire, is lower in resistance than the cell material being bombarded by light, then electrons can be forced to flow through the wire.

Photoelectrical events generally involve very low levels of electrical energy—trickles, not raging torrents. When the event occurs there is no way to detect its occurrence without a means of picking up the minute quantity of excited electrons. Laboratory equipment properly set up can be used to detect the photoelectrical effect, but without accurate instrumentation capable of extraordinarily sensitive measurements it is very difficult to know exactly what is happening and what quantities are involved. This is the primary reason why no one fully understood the photoelectric phenomenon until recently, even though it was observed by the French scientist Edmond Becquerel in 1839 while he was experimenting with battery-like devices. Later in the nineteenth century, usually while experimenting with photoelectric events for different reasons, other scientists noted the same phenomenon but saw little immediate use for the knowledge. In 1954 scientists at Bell Labs, while doing experimental work on semiconductors, developed a simple silicon photovoltaic cell that generated a higher quantity of electricity than they had thought possible. Although they understood the potential significance of this discovery, the world at that time was far too interested in other technologies, such as nuclear power, to pay any attention to what was considered an insignificant source of energy—solar power.

As noted, silicon is the primary ingredient of most photovoltaic cells now produced. Silicon's excellent capability as a semiconductor is the primary reason why it is the basic material of most photovoltaic cells. A *semiconductor* is semiconductive of electrons, or electricity. Gold and copper are excellent conductors owing to their low resistance to electrical flow. By comparison silicon is much less conductive; it is closer to being a ceramic material than a metal.

Silicon is an element second only to oxygen in abundance; it accounts for about a quarter of the Earth's crust. Silicon is readily available in its raw state as silica quartz, or sand, which is mined in conventional mining operations. Silica is a primary constituent of more than 95 percent of the rocks on Earth. The glare of sunlight off quartz crystal grains in the white sands of many beaches visibly confirms the abundant presence of silicon.

Prior to 1787, the few scientists who had investigated silica assumed that it was an element and had no other constituents. Lavoisier, in 1787, made an educated guess that silica sand was actually an oxide of some element as yet undiscovered. Thirty-six years later, in 1823, the scientist Berzelius "cracked" silica into its constituents, one part silicon and two parts oxygen, and created the first actual piece of silicon. In 1854, the French chemist H. Sainte-Claire Deville developed the first workable means of refining silica into pure silicon. Pure silicon turned out to be a dullish gray substance that looks and feels like metal but is more closely related to diamonds than steel. Pure silicon has a crystal atomic structure of diamond form, and it melts at a very high temperature—more than 2500 degrees Fahrenheit.

While silicon appears dense and rigid, there is considerable space between its atomic components; it is as solid as it is empty. Traveling through silicon on the atomic scale, we would see a matrix of atoms in all directions, each aligned with four others in a cubic pattern and all equidistant from one another. We'd see tiny electrons moving in shells, like orbits, around each nucleus, each electron in perfect equilibrium with its neighbors. As we traveled through this lattice of diamond-locked nuclei, all electrons would

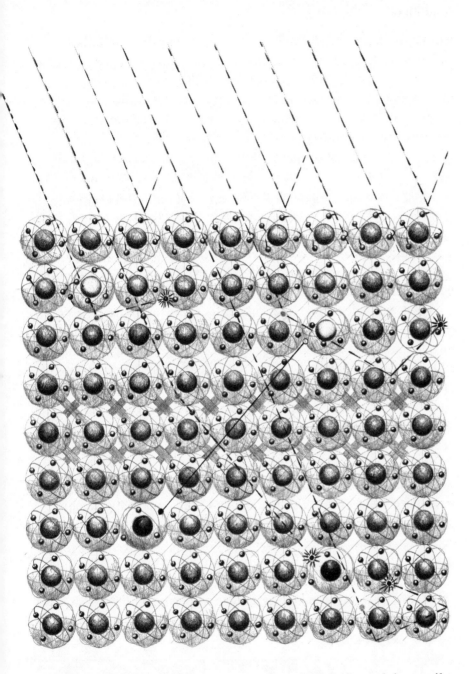

A cross-section of a crystalline silicon cell. The barrier layer, or junction, is visible across the center. Sunlight strikes from top left. The first photon displaces an electron, which goes off seeking a vacant orbit about a nucleus. The second photon knocks free an electron, which travels through the junction and is seen passing a three-electron boron atom. The third photon bounces off, as many do. The fourth makes a straight dash all the way to the backing at lower right, and is reflected back until it crashes into an electron. The fifth knocks an electron into movement. The sixth bounces off. The seventh and eighth have yet to strike electrons, and the ninth is reflected.

In the top layer, there are two light nuclei with five electrons, phosphorus, and in the bottom there are two dark nuclei, boron, with three electrons. When the cell is made, the instant the second impurity, phosphorus, is added, the junction is formed. At that instant, the extra electrons in phosphorus atoms that are close to the junction (solid line) leap across the zone of static electricity to fill the void created by three-electron boron atoms in a four-electron silicon matrix.

be essentially stable in their movement around their nuclei—until struck by a source of light.

Photons that have traveled 93,000,000 miles from the sun streak through silicon like meteors. Inevitably, some of these photons strike electrons, causing them to rebound in a new direction. Less one electron, the nucleus is like a car wheel that has lost its counterweight and is out of balance. Where the electron was there is a vacant hole; an orbiting electron is required for stability but it has been knocked out of orbit by a photon. As the lattice of silicon is bombarded by billions of photons, millions of electrons are displaced and sent into a chaotic dance through the lattice.

In our journey among the nuclei, we would see electrons darting past in all directions, and flashes all around us as photons crashed into electrons. As each electron lost its energy, it would start being pulled into vacant orbits, one after another until finally its energy would be so weak it would be captured in the orbit of a nucleus. If the source of light were blocked and the stream of photons stopped, all electrons would be immediately caught by nuclei and equilibrium would be established. In essence this sequence of events is the photoelectrical effect, the excitation of electrons by the bombardment of photons.

Heat will cause much the same effect. For example, if a steel rod is evenly heated electrons will become active; enough heat will turn the steel molten and the electrons will be dancing about feverishly as the steel begins to flow like a liquid. On the other hand, if only one end of the steel rod is heated, the other end remaining cool, the electrons will tend to migrate from the hot end to the cold end. The imbalance will force movement of electrons, therefore heat, from one end to the other.

Crystalline silicon. Like most semiconductive materials, it is composed of atoms aligned in a perfect cubic pattern, a diamond structure. Polycrystalline silicon is usually cast or grown through a die; thus the crystal formation tends to occur in clusters. The surface of a polycrystalline cell often looks like petrified particleboard. Amorphous is chaotic; the atomic structure is not orderly.

Pure silicon would not cause a photovoltaic effect by itself simply because all the electrons are in balance. An intentional state of imbalance must be created, analogous to one end of the steel rod being in a fire and the other being in a refrigerator. Within the silicon photovoltaic cell there must be a state of imbalance to force the electrons, in their tendency to seek equilibrium, to move through a wire beyond the cell itself. So, the trick in making a photovoltaic cell lies in adding minute impurities—measured in parts per *billion*—to the silicon to create what might be called a

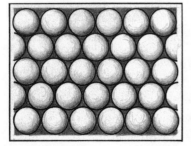
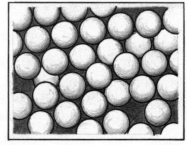
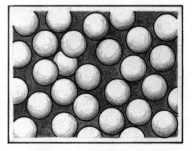

state of constant dynamic imbalance.

In the production of PVs extremely pure silicon is melted in a crucible within a furnace until it is white hot. A minute quantity of boron is added to the silicon. A special metal rod attached to a cable is slowly lowered into the pool. Although the rod is hot, it is considerably cooler than the silicon-boron mix. As the rod is slowly drawn back up out of the pool, silicon-boron atoms begin to cool and solidify around the rod in a crystalline pattern. After the rod has been raised well above the pool, the molten silicon-boron mix continues to congeal into a solid red-hot mass, like gooey taffy or hardcandy being pulled from a pot atop the stove. Gradually, over a period of hours, an ingot shaped like a salami is "grown" from the molten pool. Once the ingot is completely cooled it can be sliced into thin wafers which will eventually become complete photovoltaic cells.

Cabinetmakers cut hardwood with thin-bladed high-quality saws. They must make very precise judgments about the depth and position of the cut to allow for the saw's width—called the *kerf*. Semiconductor and photovoltaic manufacturers have agonized over the problem of kerf, and how to minimize it, because silicon is expensive to produce and slicing it into wafers to make cells often results in substantial material losses in the form of very expensive sawdust. The primary method in use involves a gang saw of very strong thin wires laid across the silicon ingot, which is laid within a bath of slurry containing fine abrasive particles. Like a hundred knives cutting through a salami at once, the saw blades are carefully moved back and forth across the silicon until the entire ingot is sliced into hair-thin wafers.

Other simpler and more efficient techniques of manufacturing cells are showing promise, both in reducing losses due to kerf and accelerating the production process. Ribbon cells, analogous to drawing ribbon candy from a pot, can be made by pulling the silicon from the crucible through a precisely shaped die. The die forms the cell's basic shape, thus eliminating entirely the step of sawing cells from a solid ingot. Mobil Solar Energy Corporation has taken this process a step further, with substantial reductions in cost, by developing a technique of pulling ribbons as a nine-sided tube—a nonagon. The thin-walled tube is drawn through a special die located just above the molten pool of silicon. The completed tube is then sliced into square wafers by a laser—an application of light to cut wafers that will receive light to generate electricity.

In addition to ingot and ribbon techniques of producing crystalline silicon, there are two other primary techniques involving polycrystalline and amorphous silicon. Silicon melted and simply poured into a mold, as one might mold a metal or plastic, can result in a polycrystalline cell of lower cost, and lower efficiency, compared to crystalline. At still lower efficiency and cost, amorphous silicon—which is noncrystalline and thus internally "jumbled"—can be deposited in very thin layers on a variety of materials. The backing material, or substrate, is passed through a vacuum chamber containing silicon in a plasma state—a very hot gas. Particles of silicon adhere to the substrate like dust settling on a smooth surface.

In the more common production methods, once the ribbons or wafers have been made, they are polished to a glassy surface with the top left exposed and the bottom bonded to a foil-like conductive metal. The bottom surface then becomes both a conductor and an impermeable surface.

Rainwater falling on bone-dry desert sandstone will permeate down into the stone, but only so far. The water molecules will reach a point within the granular structure of the stone where there is insufficient pressure from above to force the water any further. More rain will be blocked by the water already contained in the stone and it will run off.

Silicon cells, doped with an impurity of boron and coated on one side with metal foil, must be doped with a second impurity if a state of dynamic imbalance is to be created within the cell. But like the sandstone absorbing water, this second impurity must only go so far within the silicon; it cannot go all the way to the bottom. Phosphorus is a commonly used element in silicon cells as the second doping impurity.

Hot silicon cells passing through a special furnace are exposed to phosphorus gas for a very brief and precisely measured time. The period is just long enough for a minute quantity of phosphorus to permeate the upper regions of each cell without permeating the entire cell or entering through the bottom. In the millisecond in which the phosphorus enters the silicon-boron cell, a state of dynamic imbalance is instantaneously created. The entire concept of photovoltaic cells relies upon this totally natural, instantaneous, and nearly miraculous event.

The scale on which the permeation of phosphorus—and indeed much of the entire silicon-cell-manufacturing process—occurs is so miniscule that dimensions are commonly expressed in angstroms, a unit of measurement normally used to measure the wavelength of radiation. An angstrom is equal to one hundred-millionth of a centimeter.

The diffusion of phosphorus into silicon cells causes what is referred to as the barrier layer to occur. It is the region where the upper silicon-boron-phosphorus layer blends with the lower silicon-boron layer. The barrier layer is charged with static electricity—if it were not, the photovoltaic cell would not work. The barrier layer cannot be seen—there is nothing there to see—and it cannot be created except by an extraordinarily precise diffusion of phosphorus, or a similar element, into the silicon. Too much or too little phosphorus will dramatically alter the cell's functioning. Given this almost unbelievably subtle effect within the barrier layer, and the extremely fine tolerances required to sustain cell manufacture, it is obvious why photovoltaic production was practically out of the question prior to the advent of contemporary computers and high-resolution methods of measurement.

A muddy river flowing into the blue sea is of a different viscosity and temperature than the sea. From a cliff above the beach, one can see a line between brown and blue water, distinct near the river's mouth and gradually merging as one looks farther out. This is a zone of turbulence, of static. It is a barrier layer.

The silicon atom has four electrons in its outermost shell, boron has three electrons, and phosphorus has five. The boron and phosphorus atoms are similar enough to silicon atoms that they fit within the diamond crystal lattice, but since they have different numbers of electrons, a degree of imbalance is created. Boron results in empty holes, or orbits, where there are too few electrons to achieve equilibrium, and phosphorus causes similar imbalances because there are too many electrons.

In that millisecond in which phosphorus enters the hot silicon cell, only so many phosphorus atoms have time to seek locations in the silicon-boron wafer. As they come to rest, the extra phosphorus electron tends to seek the nearest vacant orbit in a boron atom, since the boron atom only has three electrons and—within a matrix of silicon atoms, each with four electrons—is out of balance. In the upper layer, permeated with phosphorus, all the empty orbits are filled with electrons that have migrated from phosphorus atoms to boron atoms, so the imbalance is corrected. Just below the area of permeated silicon, at the point where the phosphorus atoms have stopped their travel into the silicon, the phosphorus atoms lose one electron to the boron atoms below, becoming positively charged in the process. The boron atoms that have captured the free electrons become negatively charged. A zone of static electricity, the barrier layer, is the result. It is a permanent feature of the cell and insofar as anyone knows will not change for the lifetime of the cell—greater than fifteen years.

The static barrier layer is like a filter between the top (n) layer composed of silicon-boron-phosphorus and the bottom (p) layer composed of just silicon-boron. Photons can pass through this filtering barrier, but only the most highly charged electrons—those with the greatest energy—can pass through the static.

Were we to travel into the cell's top n layer, we would see photons striking electrons and sending them off in chaotic paths seeking empty orbits in the lattice. But since the phosphorus atoms have already yielded their extra electrons to fill vacant boron orbits, there are few holes to fill. Photons keep striking electrons on down into the barrier layer, but throughout the n layer the electron movement is so dense that each electron tends to have too little energy and to be traveling at too slow a rate to break through the barrier-layer static and reach empty orbits below. Instead, they rebound back into the chaos of the n layer. As we would see if we passed into the p layer, photons continue to strike electrons, but in this region, since there are no phosphorus atoms present, there are many more empty orbits. Electrons struck by photons are broken from their orbits, in silicon or boron atoms, and quickly find equilibrium. As a result, there is less chaotic electron movement, each electron bounds about for less time, and as a consequence many are traveling at higher energy levels than their counterparts in the n layer above. Many have enough energy to crash through the barrier layer, adding their presence to the already chaotic crush of electrons seeking equilibrium, but are unable to find a vacant orbit. Looking across the barrier layer into the upper n layer, we see a dizzying, chaotic dance of electrons rushing about through the lattice. This is the state of dynamic imbalance.

Atop the cell, a web of silvery flat wires spans the surface like the veins of a leaf. They cover only a minimum of the cell's surface so as to not block incoming photons. Since the wire is metal, it is far more conductive than silicon and therefore it provides an escape route for the pressurized electrons within the silicon lattice. Beneath the cell, the bottom p layer is coated with metallic foil, also conductive. Once the top wires are connected to the bottom metallic foil by a wire, a circuit is completed. Electrons will then flow out of the top n layer, through the wire, and back into the lower p layer in a continual attempt to seek equilibrium by filling the empty orbits—as long as the light shines.

One or two of these cells might supply sufficient energy to power a small radio, wristwatch, or other consumer product, but in most applications cells are linked together into modules of ten, twenty, or forty cells. Modules are then linked by wire into arrays, covering a roof or mounted on a fixed panel. If the cell is a leaf, the module is a branch, and the array is the tree. A single cell, a single module, or an entire array is wired into a circuit—that is, a loop of electrical current—and various appliances can then be plugged into the circuit. Depending on the system's configuration and purpose, it may also include an inverter to convert direct current from the cells into alternating current, a power-conditioning unit that modulates the output of power into a steady flow regardless of the sunlight's intensity, and a set of deep-cycle batteries to store electricity for non-sunny periods.

One photovoltaic cell is capable of generating enough electricity to energize an electric motor the size of a spool of thread. It is possible to purchase one cell, a few pieces of wiring, and a small electric motor for about $20. Wire the cell and motor together, place the cell in direct sunlight, and the motor will start when the sun comes up, stopping when it goes down. The first rays of morning sunshine will cause the motor to barely turn; as the sun rises the motor will reach top speed, which it will maintain from midmorning to midafternoon, finally slowing to a stop as the sun sets. If a cloud passes in front of the sun, the motor will slow but not stop. If the day is stormy and dark, the motor will slow even more, but it will not stop for there is still sufficient sunlight. Day in and day out, the motor will start and stop with the sun for ten, twenty, maybe thirty years. During that time it will require little or no attention, it will make no smoke and no noise, and it will not require any fuel—except pure unadulterated, natural, nonsynthetic, organic sunlight.

The Modularity of Photovoltaic Cells

A single photovoltaic cell is analogous to a single coin: one is a unit of power, and ten equals ten times the power of one unit. PV cells or amorphous photovoltaic panels can be clustered into modules of convenient size. The modules can in turn be clustered into larger arrays composed of dozens, hundreds, or thousands of modules. Arrays, as groups of modules lined up in rows, can be arranged in vast fields. At each scale of use the single cell or single amorphous panel remains just as efficient on its own as it does as a unit amidst a field of thousands. Thus, PVs are inherently modular and infinitely arrangeable to suit every conceivable scale of operation, from fueling a child's toy to a 100-megawatt power plant.

As Section I suggested, this inherent difference between photovoltaic technology and all other forms of electrical generation has profound implications for the industry's development, marketing strategies, global potential, and research approach. Practically all conventional forms of electrical generation, including renewable technologies such as small-scale hydropower and wind generators, have very specific optimum scales at which they are most efficient. Large coal and nuclear plants must be constructed as specialized facilities; their technology does not lend itself to mass production of entire plants. Unlike all other technologies, photovoltaics are modular. The same cell used in a child's toy can be manufactured in sufficient numbers to electrify a thousand houses.

ARCO Solar's marketing of its standard PV module, approximately 40 watts peak output, demonstrates the implications of inherently modular photovoltaics. The same module has been used on backwoods cabins in northern California and in the first major utility application of photovoltaics—a 1-megawatt central power station now operating east of Los Angeles. Furthermore, the same module is now operating at remote sites requiring electricity at practically all imaginable levels from 40 watts on up to 1 kilowatt.

The inherently modular nature of photovoltaics has undoubtedly been a major factor in the dramatic drop in prices since the

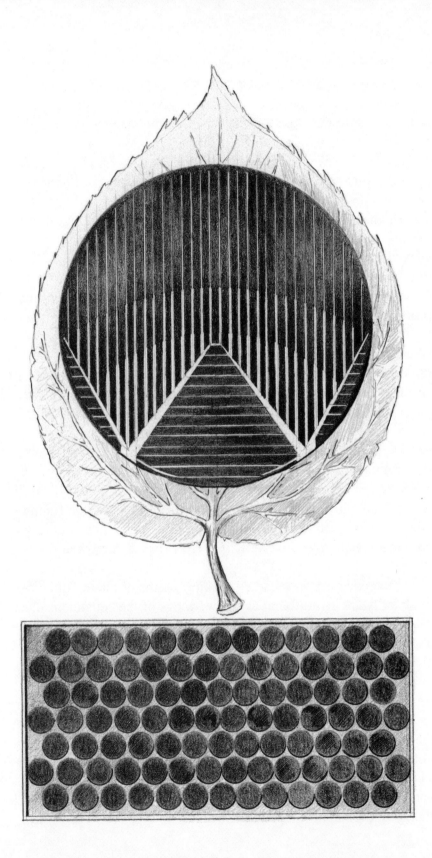

A round or square cell, analogous to a veined leaf. The assemblage of cells is called a module and modules can be grouped into arrays—clusters of modules. The module is the branch, an array the tree. The intrinsic beauty of photovoltaic technology lies in the cells' look—the veinlike, leaflike appearance—and their inherent modularity.

early 1970s, and it will continue to result in production efficiencies. The research and development process behind the evolution of practically all conventional electrical-generating systems has involved improvements to thousands of components—valves, boilers, piping systems, generators, controls, and so on. The efficiency and economic values of the technology are to a great extent reliant upon the simultaneous improvement of a wide variety of components and design strategies. Even the lowly diesel electric generator, the mainstay of Third World power generation and thousands of industrial applications throughout the world, is the result of decades of innovations applied to everything from valves in the engine to cooling fins in the radiator. In many instances, the improvement of one component in the whole system, a diesel fuel injector, can result in a wide range of changes to the entire unit. Furthermore, the typical diesel generator may have components made by anywhere from ten to fifty manufacturers that the primary manufacturer must maintain in stock as replacement parts. On the scale of a standard coal-fired power plant, which has more than one hundred times the output of a typical diesel generator, the entire machine requires the maintenance of a research and development effort by dozens of companies. By comparison, the manufacture and marketing of photovoltaics requires the concentration of research and development on one basic part—the cell itself. While much research and development work has been done on module framing systems, lamination techniques to protect the cells, and a variety of production techniques, the principal effort has always been the cell itself.

The production and marketing implications of photovoltaic cell modularity are as profound as the workings of the cells themselves. They allow both a structural shift in the way electricity is generated and a shift in the way generating systems are marketed. If the efficiency and costs of generating electricity with photovoltaics are effectively the same whether the facility is a two-panel unit on a tiny house or a 1000-panel centralized utility plant, then there is no technical or economic reason why the manufacturer cannot market the same technology to both users, and every imaginable market potential between those extremes.

Oil is a fluid that can be cracked into a variety of constituents—diesel fuel, gasoline, kerosene, motor oil, butane—and each liquid or gas can be carried in tankers of all types or in pipelines.

The oil industry has developed a vast infrastructure for producing, marketing, and transporting its elementary commodities. Oil companies are accustomed to the notion of selling a basic, widely used, and extremely flexible fuel. Characteristically, oil companies view energy as a commodity that, optimally, ought to be flexible in its adaptability to a very broad range of consumer and commercial applications.

Electricity is a state of energy that, like oil, can be modulated, moved, stored, and turned off or on. But unlike oil, electricity is a second-generation energy source, given conventional means of electrical generation. A fuel is required to generate heat, to create steam, and to drive a turbine and generator. Given the losses that are inevitable in the transformation of oil, gas, and coal into electrical energy, coupled with the technical complexity of power plants necessary to make the transformation, the generation of electrical energy by conventional means has become a highly sophisticated and specialized business unto itself. Design firms such as Bechtel and Fluor, often working in partnership with such corporations as General Electric and Westinghouse, represent a substantial industry whose primary focus is the design and construction of large-scale, centralized electrical generating facilities—electron factories.

In the mid-seventies, many oil companies began to explore and invest in various solar and renewable technologies. Some made substantial moves into solar hot-water heating by purchasing small companies that had pioneered the technology; others became involved as joint-venture partners in various geothermal, wind-power, and small-scale hydroelectric projects. With few exceptions, the oil industry has backed off from these endeavors. In the case of solar-water heating, oil companies found they did not have the expertise to engage in a business that was more closely related to the plumbing and building trades than to supplying basic forms of energy. And in the case of more place-specific and specialized power plants, oil companies are often ill-equipped to deal with the wide range of unknowns that are the inevitable result of such inherently "local" technology. Generally, and with few exceptions, the oil companies are too large, and too accustomed to providing what is essentially a fluid commodity, to engage in businesses involving the development of complex manufacturing processes or highly place-specific and specialized technology.

In the mid-seventies various editorials in the energy-business trade press, and in the media at large, made cynical comments about the oil industry relative to solar energy. The gist of their commentary: the oil companies won't invest in solar because they can't buy the sun. A few years later, as it became apparent that oil companies were buying up practically every photovoltaic firm in sight, the same editorial writers often implied, or directly stated, their belief that "BIG OIL" would buy out the solar-energy industry and restrain its growth in relation to their primary oil business.

Such commentary certainly expressed a very real frustration with the often glacial movement of large corporations, but it also ignored some elemental facts. A small company with perhaps $10 million in annual revenue and 20 employees can drop an entire product line and shift its entire strategy within one meeting of its management and a few months of painful change. An oil company with billions in annual revenue and 50,000 to 75,000 employees, not to mention millions of shareholders and decades of blue-chip stock performance, must take years of careful planning even to begin a shift in product and service orientation. Oil companies, as well as the oil industry taken as a whole, simply cannot move quickly into a new area lest they incur the wrath of stockholders and generate organizational problems that could prove fatal.

These organizational problems aside, the oil companies represent a huge enterprise built upon a vanishing substance. In their tentative explorations in renewables and solar technology in the mid-seventies they were like brontosaurs attempting to survive on dry weeds after having eaten all the trees. While it is tempting to assume that these massive organizations are so all powerful they can afford to "lock up solar energy" by buying photovoltaics producers, such an assumption ignores the fact that oil companies are hunting for a means of survival. They are not interested in dabbling in energy politics, but in finding and developing a technology that will allow their continued existence. The criteria for this new technology: huge market, long-term growth, strong alignment with a wide range of social and economic trends, and, preferably, sufficient modularity that the technology becomes analogous to oil.

Regardless of one's personal bias about oil companies, or large corporations in general, it is impossible to deny that the essential nature of photovoltaics fits the oil industry's objectives like a glove. Like oil, photovoltaics can be mass produced—as cells and modules—and sold to every imaginable customer from individuals to small groups to whole towns to utility companies to corporations. And from the oil company's point of view, photovoltaics offer a long-term potential that suggests the probable replacement not only of oil but of coal and nuclear as well. This is all the more meaningful when one realizes that oil was replacing coal until the 1970s, when the energy crisis resulted in a massive shift to coal, which was cheaper and could be obtained domestically, and nuclear was beginning to cut into both oil and coal markets as fuel for utility-scale electrical generation. So, at least potentially, the entry of oil companies into the photovoltaic business represents an end run around oil's primary competition.

Oil companies do not have to own the sun; all they have to do is become the providers of the device that supplies electricity transformed from solar light. In so doing they replace the fuel, and the concept of fuel, with an elegantly simple means of generation that is saleable practically everywhere on Earth, almost regardless of language, sophistication, scale of need, and availability of resources.

Photovoltaic Industry: The Players

In 1983, Atlantic Richfield Company generated revenues totaling $25.9 billion. The corporation's 1983 annual report is dominated by photographs of various petroleum, chemical, and mining activities and only one photograph, small, of its photovoltaic cells. The photovoltaic subsidiary, ARCO Solar Incorporated, is so small in comparison with the company's petroleum, mining, chemical, and metals activities that it does not even rate a distinction in the financial statements. It is simply lumped in the "other" category. In the words of a Mobil Solar Energy Corporation management person, whose company is similarly miniscule compared with Mobil's vast and diversified operations, their subsidiary is "rounded off." The photovoltaic revenues are so small, below the hundreds of millions that justify a line in the balance sheet, they're rounded off in the translation from figures like $21,467,498,321 to those like $21.5 (in billions). This underscores the fact that even a 1 percent share of the world's energy business can be a multibillion dollar business.

Atlantic Richfield's corporate strategy takes four basic directions that typify the oil industry's overall strategy and the trends they must respond to. First, the oil industry is faced with oil prices that are essentially flat or declining, while the exploration and development of new oil sources are generally more expensive as each successive discovery is made in increasingly more remote or difficult circumstances. So the need is to maximize production from existing oil fields. Second, the industry must continue to locate and develop new sources of oil and natural gas at the lowest possible risk. Third, in recognizing the declining value of oil products through conservation and the development of alternatives, the industry must maximize its utilization of its existing technology and organizational resources. And fourth, the industry must diversify away from total dependence on petroleum. In short, the industry is focused on becoming lean, efficient, and responsive—like the small cars their gasoline powers—while simultaneously beginning the development of technologies that will, in all probability,

U.S. Photovoltaic Industry 1983

Company or Program	Number	Sales
Module Manufacturers Companies who assemble modules as well as make cells and modules	11 companies	$76 million
Research and development programs Corporations engaged in developing technology but not necessarily committed on a long-term basis to PV production	12 (major)	$25 million
System integrators Companies that buy all the components and put them together for a specific project/client	45	$170 million
Material suppliers Companies that supply basic materials for PV production or are engaged in developing new materials and module components	11	$30 million
Manufacturing equipment Companies that build machines for making photovoltaic cells and modules	5	$4 million
Balance of system components Companies that make inverters, metering equipment, batteries, and small packaged systems	12	$40 million
Estimated total sales:		*$345 million*
Estimated employees:	96 companies, 4000–6000 people	

(Source: Strategies Unlimited, Congressional Testimony, Sept. 1984 used by permission)

replace oil within two to three decades as the industry's primary source of revenue.

ARCO Solar may be a small subsidiary of Atlantic Richfield but it is the largest producer of photovoltaics in the United States. In 1983, ARCO shipped 6 megawatts of photovoltaics out into the world. Of that total, 4.5 megawatts went the short distance northward from ARCO's plant in the Los Angeles area to a new utility-scale facility now operating near Bakersfield, California.

The bulk of ARCO's output is single-crystal silicon cells in 40-watt modules. In 1984, the company announced their entry into the amorphous-silicon field by displaying a new amorphous panel for small-scale uses such as recharging boat and recreational vehicle batteries. While ARCO Solar maintains what is perhaps the largest privately financed research team in the world, their work has been

Solarwest Electric of Santa Barbara is an ARCO Solar distributor offering packaged systems. This is a 360-watt system designed to complement a conventional gas or diesel generator. The two sources can be used to their fullest advantage if the generator is used only for peak-load periods. This system contains twelve modules, eight batteries, one metered control panel, one inverter, one battery charger, and one transfer switch.

(Source: Solarwest Electric)

Detail view of United Energy Corporation's concentrating photovoltaic unit. The shiny glass surface is a fresnel lens, which focuses sunlight onto a PV cell about the size of a thumbnail. Cells and lenses are mounted in aluminum boxes that tilt relative to the sun's position—winter to summer—and the entire assemblage turns on a track to follow the sun from morning to evening. The water-carrying hose is visible at the lower left. Just behind the tiny cell is a small tube that carries water. Excess heat generated by the sunlight concentrated on the cell is drawn away by the water.

(Source: United Energy Corporation)

less focused on "pure" research in photovoltaic cells than on production techniques and the technology of utility-scale photovoltaic systems, which they have pioneered.

In the late 1970s, one of the most peculiar and ironic market potentials practically fell into ARCO's lap. Hundreds of backwoods residents, most living in the mountains of Northern California, began to purchase photovoltaic panels. At the time, ARCO was the only major producer with a dependable and accessible panel available through local distributors. Since many of the backwoods residents were growing certain illicit crops, cash was not an obstacle. Cash flowed, and ARCO Solar was off the ground.

On the basis of megawatts produced in 1983, the United Energy Corporation, based in the San Francisco Bay Area, is the second largest photovoltaic producer—4.5 megawatts in 1983. UEC was founded in 1978 by Ernest Lampert, and is probably one of the most unique, visionary, and innovative companies in the photovoltaic industry. The company's accomplishments, in a mere seven years, would be a challenge to a major corporation let alone a fledgling operation that barged into the capital-intensive energy

A single UEC module set on a circular pond. As the sun's position changes during the day, the module rolls around the pond's periphery. The weight of the module is supported by foam floats on the water, thus reducing the weight-transfer problems associated with the slow transport of an unwieldy framework.

(Source: United Energy Corporation)

industry practically out of thin air.

Advocates of renewable energy often refer to fossil fuels as the energy "capital" of the planet Earth and solar energy as the energy "income." While this is a useful analogy, it has rarely been translated into action so effectively as by the United Energy Corporation. UEC is involved in photovoltaics, the generation of thermal energy in the form of hot water for building heat and industrial processes, the creation of food-producing ponds and fields, distillation of plant material into ethanol for use as a motor fuel, and the integration of all these functions into total systems. Unlike most photovoltaic producers, UEC has successfully focused on whole systems in which photovoltaics are a primary component, not just an add-on technology.

UEC's primary product is a photovoltaic module that uses concentrating lenses to increase the sun's input to each cell and thus increases efficiency. Typically, concentrating photovoltaic systems can result in dramatic gains in efficiency—between 9–15 and 15–20 percent for standard crystalline cells—with relatively minor changes in cell structure and cost. However, the primary problem with concentrating cells is that they must be precisely focused upon the sun at all times. The second problem is the heat generated by the intense concentration of energy—the cell is analogous in design to a magnifying glass focused on a leaf. UEC's 5000DX module, its basic unit, consists of an array of concentrator cells set on a frame above a pond of water. The entire array slowly tracks the sun by rolling on the rim of the pond. The water is circulated through the concentrator modules, drawing the heat away in the process. The result: power output of 2.5 kilowatts of electricity *and* 40,000 BTU per hour of heat via the hot water.

Unfortunately UEC's dramatic growth has come to an abrupt halt. In 1984 the Internal Revenue Service began investigating the company for an alleged fraudulent investment scheme. Even though *no* guilt has been established, the mere mention of UEC's name on an IRS document, one that was supposed to be for internal IRS use only but was somehow released, was enough to scare investors away. So its pioneering efforts become moot in the face of unsubtantiated allegations made in the press and by the IRS. The company is now suing the IRS while practically functioning at a maintenance level with a fraction of its previous staff. The tragedy is the loss of jobs and progress in photovoltaic technology.

Solarex Corporation of Rockville, Maryland, is the third largest photovoltaic manufacturer in the United States. Solarex sold 1.3 megawatts of polycrystal cells in 1983, primarily for a wide variety of home and industrial applications. Solarex is a pioneer in the PV industry, having developed the first polycrystal PV module in widespread use. Polycrystal involves casting silicon rather than drawing it from a molten pool. While the efficiency of polycrystal is somewhat lower than single crystal, it is considerably cheaper to produce. In the early 1980s, Solarex also constructed the world's first solar "breeder" factory, a PV factory operated entirely with a 200-kilowatt PV-power system that is also the building's roof. Solarex modules also power a wide variety of structures, including a gas station in Chicago, the Oklahoma Center for Science and Arts in Oklahoma City, and the world's first full-scale home installation, a demonstration house in Carlisle, Massachusetts. In 1983, Solarex acquired RCA's amorphous-photovoltaic operation and is now engaged in perfecting this technology for mass production. Solarex is partially owned by Standard Oil of Indiana.

Mobil Solar Energy Corporation of Waltham, Massachusetts, is

The elegance of the photovoltaic product, here expressed in Mobil's square poly-crystalline cells, made by the unique "nona-gon" growth process. The nonagon (center) results from drawing molten silicon through a nine-faceted die. A laser is used to slice the nonagon into squares, which are then polished and coated with a thin matrix of wires on one side and a solid metallic backing film on the other.

(Source: Mobil Solar Energy Corporation)

not a major producer of PVs, not yet, but it has completed major research towards the development of low-cost ribbon-grown cells. It was Mobil that developed the technique allowing a nonagonal (nine–sided) tube to be drawn from a molten pool of silicon. The completed tube is then sliced into small squares, which are placed in rows to form a complete module. Mobil's "Ra" modules have been used as power sources for houses, pipeline cathodic protection, water pumping, and desalinization, and they have been sold with a total lighting package as exterior streetlight systems requiring no external utility hookups. Mobil's commitment to solar energy as a long-term investment is evidenced by the depth and quality of its research effort.

Solavolt International of Phoenix, Arizona, is the result of a partnership between Motorola, the electronics manufacturer, and SES Inc., a subsidiary of Shell Oil Company. Solavolt produces PV modules composed of polycrystalline cells. The company is now exploring new ribbon-production techniques.

Solenergy Corporation of Woburn, Massachusetts, is a producer of conventional single-crystal PVs in module form. Increas-

---

World Photovoltaic Supply and Where It Goes

1983: Total production 15.6 megawatts (Mw)
United States total: 9.6 Mw
5.5 Mw: Tax credit projects of all types and sizes
3.4 Mw: Commercial sales, government sales
      1.6 : Domestic
      1.8 : Exported
       .1 : Exported as government aid

Japan total: 3.3 Mw
2.1 Mw: Calculators, watches and other consumer products
 .6 Mw: Government aid programs
 .6 Mw: Commercial
      .25: Domestic use
      .35: Export

Europe total: 2.4 Mw
1.2 Mw: Commercial
      .4 : Domestic use
      .8 : Export
1.2 Mw: Government
      .6 : Government foreign aid programs
      .6 : Internal use

(Source: Strategies Unlimited, Congressional Testimony, Sept. 1984 used by permission)

Production by all other countries: .3 Mw

ingly, Solenergy is focusing on custom applications, designing PV modules and whole systems for specific applications. In November 1984, Solenergy announced its signing of a portentous letter of intent with the Tianjin No. 2 Semiconductor Manufacturing Plant in the city of Tianjin, People's Republic of China. Solenergy will manufacture cells and modules in China using Tianjin's facilities and resources. A joint venture to produce PVs for the world market is also being explored.

Applied Solar, City of Industry, California (Los Angeles), is one of the more unusual photovoltaic manufacturers. Applied Solar is not only a pioneer in photovoltaics, having been in the business for twenty-five years, but it remains a primary supplier of PVs for satellites. Indeed, without Applied Solar's products, many of our long-distance phone calls would not be possible. The company also produces a wide range of concentrating and large-area cells, including tiny concentrating cells no bigger than a fingernail. Applied Solar had intended to enter the business of terrestrial photovoltaics, but at the time of this writing the company is returning to its primary focus, space, on the assumption that the federal solar

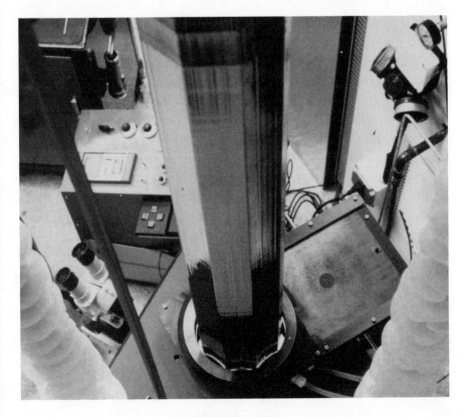

Growing a "nonagon" photovoltaic crystal. The tubular shape is being slowly withdrawn from a crucible of molten silicon. At left is a microscope for checking the formation of the nonagon as it is drawn, or grown.

(Source: Mobil Solar Energy Corporation)

tax credit will not be extended beyond December of 1985. Federal and some state tax credit programs have been major factors in encouraging sales and thus spurring the industry's growth.

Tideland Signal Corporation of Houston, Texas, is another pioneer in photovoltaics. The firm was founded in 1954 to manufacture electronic beacons and related navigational aids. In 1972, it produced the first solar-powered navigational aid lighting system— installed in the Gulf of Mexico. Tideland now manufactures very high quality single-crystal cells and a broad range—more than 200 separate products—of light and sound navigational aids powered by the sun. Tideland-built buoys now guard hundreds of harbor entrances, shipping channels, and docking facilities. The company's PV generator systems also power numerous oil and gas industry remote facilities, as well as railroad and telecommunications facilities.

Energy Conversion Devices (ECD), of Troy, Michigan, is a pioneer in the development of amorphous photovoltaics and production machinery. ECD, founded in 1960 by Stanford R. Ovshinsky, is one of the most diverse and exciting companies in the PV industry. ECD's pioneering research in the very concept of amorphous atomic structure, basic physics, has resulted in a boggling array of new products and potential new industries. In partnership with Sharp Electronics of Japan, ECD developed and built the first automated amorphous photovoltaic production facility. The machine is now producing amorphous cells for Sharp's line of electronic consumer products. Growing from their work in amorphous materials, ECD has developed a wholly new battery technology; called Ovonic batteries, these new devices promise substantial improvements in battery efficiency and storage capacity. Another product, called the OTEG, is a remarkably simple looking yet very sophisticated semiconductor device that, like PVs convert light into electricity, converts heat directly into electricity. An OTEG can, for example, be placed in the side of a wood stove and it will generate electricity. ECD is also involved in amorphous coatings for tools, drills for example, that increase their useful life up to ten times. ECD recently installed the first full-scale amorphous PV manufacturing facility in Troy, Michigan, a partnership with Standard Oil of Ohio.

Chronar Corporation of Princeton, New Jersey, is both a pioneer in amorphous photovoltaic development and, potentially, a seller of whole amorphous photovoltaic manufacturing plants. At the time of this writing Chronar is completing construction of their first full-scale amorphous manufacturing facility in Port Jervis, New York. The company has recently entered into an agreement with AFG Industries, a glass manufacturer, to build a 1-megawatt amorphous PV manufacturing plant. In another agreement, with Alabama Power and Light, a major southeastern U.S. utility, Chronar has initiated what may be the first agreement with a major utility to market photovoltaics. Until recently, Chronar was engaged in research and development work, and in 1984 they introduced small amorphous photovoltaic panels for battery charging. Perhaps the most profound implication of Chronar's work is its development of a process for laying down a thin coating of amorphous PV material on glass. In effect this means that an existing product, common float glass, is manufactured with a coating thinner than paper that will generate approximately 5 watts of electricity per square foot.

In addition to these companies, a variety of other corporations are involved in various phases of photovoltaic development. Westinghouse is perhaps the most notable, with a major research and development effort now focused on amorphous PV cells. In Japan, fifteen companies are involved in PV development and manufacture. Sanyo is the major producer, followed by Sharp and Fuji. Hoxan, a major Japanese player, is soon to establish itself in the U.S. market. European companies involved in photovoltaics include Germany's Telefunken, which produced close to 1 megawatt in 1983, and Siemens. A total of twelve companies in Germany, France, Italy, Spain, Belgium, and England are now producing photovoltaics. In India there are three companies producing PVs. In Brazil one company, in Singapore one company, and in Australia a division of Tideland Signal produces photovoltaics.

The breadth of world corporate involvement in photovoltaics, while not large by income, is testament to the implications of the technology.

Sun Businesses

In the early seventies solar houses were a media fad: Sunday supplements in the metropolitan newspapers carried regular features on how the Smiths or the Browns built their solar home. There stood the family in the doorway, greeting readers with words for the skeptical, who simply could not imagine how their home could ever be a solar house. The reality of the situation was often masked by the friendly gee-we're-the-folks-next-door-who've-gone-solar tone. The reality was an energy crisis, rising energy bills, and family budgets that seemed to be devoured by every institution known to man. We all came to realize during those few years that energy was something we could use less of and that if we did we might, just might, save some money and have more "discretionary" income. We made some changes in our houses and cars or both, and we now use less energy. By 1980 the energy crisis had faded as a plethora of other crises flooded the media, and many people assumed the solar industry had faded with it. It did not.

The sun biz in 1985 is alive and vital. It is composed of five basic segments: hot-water heating, space-heating equipment, wind generation, small-scale hydro, and photovoltaics. Hot-water heating involves a wide variety of flat-plate collectors, storage tanks, and circulation systems, most of which have been developed since the early seventies. In 1976 companies making solar collectors for hot water and space heating—some systems use hot water to circulate heat through the house—sold 6 million square feet of collectors. In 1983 sales volume climbed to 22 million square feet and it still shows no signs of slowing down. In the same period a wide range of companies have designed and marketed all kinds of devices—heat-retaining shutters, double-glazed windows, heat pumps, heat exchangers, vent systems, high-efficiency wood stoves, tiles, insulation—that can be used either to reduce energy losses in a conventional house or to solarize an existing or new house. The wind-energy business has grown phenomenally—from 4 megawatts installed in 1979 to 360 megawatts in 1984, with most of the activity occurring in California wind "farms" that sell electricity to major utilities. Small-scale hydroelectric operations are steadily proliferating, both as facilities tied in with private homes and as utility-tied generating systems. The most recent entry is the photovoltaic segment, growing from 0.25 megawatts sold in 1976, yielding about $6.8 million in gross revenue, to 15 megawatts in 1983 worth over $136 million.

The total gross revenue of the entire solar and renewable industry is practically impossible to define precisely, because there is considerable overlap between products used in "solar" applications and those used simply to conserve energy in conventional homes. However, growth figures compiled by the Internal Revenue Service provide a sense of scale and hint at the real numbers, which would be quite a bit higher, since IRS figures only represent those who claimed a tax credit for a solar or conservation-related installation. In 1978 claims totaled $125 million, primarily for solar as opposed to wind and geothermal applications. By 1982 the total was $867 million, most going toward solar applications.

The five segments of the industry tend to be related to different aspects of the building trades and utility industries. Solar collectors, conservation technology, and the wide variety of devices for solarizing a home evolved as entrepreneurial efforts but soon became connected to companies involved in home and commercial building products. Wind and hydro technology is generally more sophisticated, in design and installation, than your average home-improvement device, and the technology tends to be more applicable to utility applications than to individual homes. As a result, the industry is a melding of high-technology companies, usually entrepreneurial efforts rather than older, more established firms, and firms with the financial sophistication to develop fairly large-scale wind-farm projects tied into utility grids. Conservation technology, like hot-water systems, is closely related to the building trades, and in most cases involves products and companies that are well established. Photovoltaics grew out of the high and rarified stratosphere of esoteric semiconductor research. Just as the personal computer represents the transition from a precisely defined business market to a broad consumer market, so photovoltaics represent a move from arcane scientific technology to consumer technology. Until the introduction of photovoltaic-powered water pumps in a recently announced line of solar hot-water collectors, the PV industry was somewhat distinct from the building trades. This one product, announced in 1984, signaled the integration of photovoltaics into the wide range of existing solar technologies marketed to home-owners and builders.

America is a land of do-it-yourselfers who like to spend an afternoon tinkering with new technology. Every suburban shopping area now has the 1980s equivalent of the 1940s lumber yard, though lumber is only a minor source of income there. These stores stock every imaginable gadget to solve every imaginable home-repair problem. Many of these products can be used to modify a house or small commercial building into a more efficient and ultimately solar home. In the last decade, many of these stores, previously locally owned, have become part of national chains that buy wholesale in trainload lots. The evolution of "home-improvement centers" with their own national marketing campaigns responds to a series of trends that have been quietly altering the way Americans perceive, and modify, homes. In the past fifteen years, not only have we purchased smaller cars that achieve high gas mileage but also we have kept cars longer—the average period of ownership is now about seven years. Similarly, we are now keeping homes longer while tending to modify our existing houses rather than buying new ones.

Obviously, we are in the process of improving the efficiency of homes—both financially and in terms of energy use—in the same way we have already drastically improved the efficiency of our cars. Home-improvement centers are analogous to auto supply stores. Both kinds of retail centers respond to the high cost of hiring someone to do work for us, and to the long-term trend toward keeping houses and cars longer and ensuring that their efficiency be maintained and even increased.

In addition to these basic trends, we are also responding to various social trends that are changing the very concept of a dwelling. For financial or aesthetic reasons, we are more likely to buy an old house and fix it up than simply to buy a new suburban home. In many instances this trend may be related more directly to reducing the commute distance from suburb to downtown office by buying an older home closer to the central business district than to purely aesthetic choice. In other instances the need to accommodate an elderly family member may result in the modification of an old house or the construction of a new apartment in what had been a garage or basement. Or a family might decide to rent out a spare

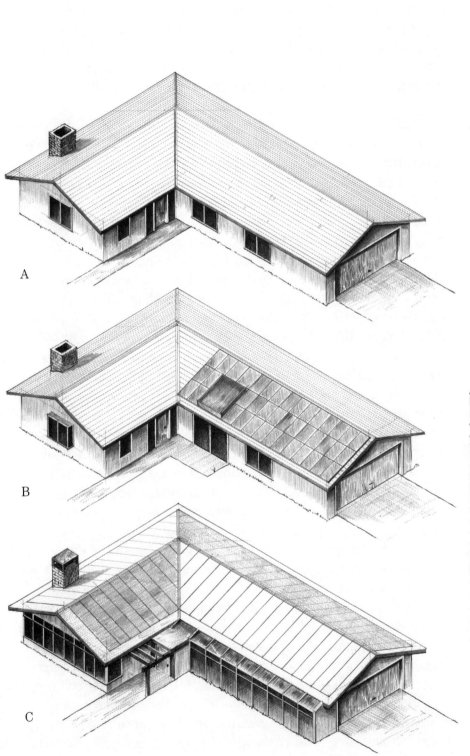

A typical suburban home (a) as it might have looked in 1970 when built. (b) Twenty years later the owner has fitted a hot-water heater and PV array on the roof and a small greenhouse bay-window unit on the home's south facing side. (c) By 2010 the house has been transformed by a full greenhouse, more south-facing glass, an entryway with double doors, and a PV roofing material. It has gone from no solar to more than half solar to 100 percent solar. One, two, or three owners have done it.

A

B

C

room to increase their income, necessitating the construction of a new doorway or kitchen. An interest in gardening may result in the construction of a greenhouse so the homeowner can have fruits and vegetables all year round. The reasons may be as varied as the living arrangements but the result is often the gradual modification of the home into a more energy efficient and potentially solar structure.

The first solar homes of the early 1970s were often freakish adaptations of conventional thinking about home architecture. Typically, these primitive structures embodied misconceptions about how a house works in the sun. As often as not these first attempts at solar architecture were the work of untrained experimenters who tended to think that a house had to look different, had to *do* something, if it was to be a solar house. As their often inventive work was subjected to the elements, builders frequently found that the elements—rain, wind, ice, and snow—have a way of rapidly exploiting every little leak and crack in a building. They realized that the sloppiness that might have been tolerable on a 1950s suburban house when oil was cheap is unacceptable in the 1980s when the price is four times higher and you're trying to capture all the solar heat you can. Builders became obsessed with details.

More people built and lived in solar homes, and at this writing there are an estimated 600,000 passive solar homes in the United States (passive systems, as opposed to active, involve only solar energy to operate, no electrical system is required). In this growth period it became obvious to most designers that a solar home was not as difficult to achieve as had been thought. Indeed, what distinguished a solar home from a conventional structure was a host of subtle, carefully worked out details, many of which were not apparent to the untrained eye. Many builders, convinced that a solar home was feasible without architectural gymnastics, set about building relatively conventional-looking homes that included a wide variety of simple strategies for capturing and retaining heat.

In designing a solar home, or increasing the efficiency of a conventional home, the first step is a detailed inventory of the building's environment, current performance, and energy requirements—space heat, hot water, cooking, refrigeration, air cooling, and electricity. The dual surprise in this process is often a recognition of just how much energy we use and how much less we really need. An inventory of a conventional home often reveals the structure to be an energy sieve with heat leaking out like smoke from burning leaves and electricity draining away through inefficient appliances—pennies steadily dropping into the garbage.

The modification of an existing home can result in a savings in heating—space and water—in excess of 50 percent. Construction of a fully solar home can reduce monthly heat energy expenditures to the zero to 10 percent range. Generally the additional cost in building a full solar home is only 5 to 15 percent over the cost of conventional construction. In 1985, a total solar home—solar space heating, water heating, and electricity—costs about 20 to 30 percent more than conventional construction. In any case, the result is a translation of a monthly bill—an operating expense contributing to the amortization of the utility facilities—into a monthly finance payment amortizing the cost of the entire house, including its energy systems. The inventory of energy usage becomes the basis for a financial-management system—an energy balance sheet that is reflected in the home's design and monthly payments.

It is unlikely that the millions of homes in the United States, and millions of commercial buildings that could utilize photovoltaic technology, if not a full range of solar heating and cooling systems, will be torn down and replaced by all-solar structures. The transformation of buildings to all-solar is basically a reconstructive and restorative process—a "retrofit," in technospeak. Already we've seen millions of central-city homes or their country counterparts gutted and restored, their exteriors preserved and their interiors modernized. The process of conversion has spawned a substantial industry of contractors, real estate developers, and small corporations whose service and product orientation is the revitalization and increased efficiency of old buildings.

When the cost of solarizing a conventional structure drops to about 3 to 8 percent of the building's cost, and the cost of a photovoltaic system adds only 9 to 15 percent more in most of the United States, it is probably inevitable that the transformation of buildings of all kinds will accelerate considerably. Estimates of the number of homes in the United States that could utilize PVs is in the 20 million range. This is not a small market. In most cases the information generated by homeowners, contractors, utility representatives, and professional consultants will represent a body of *local* knowledge, not generalized theories but locally based information about environmental conditions in particular places. Such place-specific information will result in a more accurate and relevant financial picture of real energy costs. The hidden environmental costs of conventional fossil-fuel use have no counterpart in the development of renewable energy. Aside from the potential environmental damage caused by the manufacture of some solar-energy technologies—slight overall owing to the fact that most solar technology uses a minimum of materials—there is no appreciable local environmental damage, no "other" costs to hide.

At the time of this writing, full solar homes and small solarized commercial buildings, utility-sponsored demonstration projects, and thousands of remote-site and vacation-cabin installations are scattered widely across the United States. Photovoltaic systems are distributed by marine, RV, electrical-supply, and solar-energy-equipment dealers throughout the country. Thousands of electrical and general contractors are familiar with solar-heating technology, and many are undoubtedly aware of photovoltaics through industry publications even if only a few have actually installed solar systems. A few dozen "packagers" and distributors of solar systems offer both total systems and consulting services to assist building owners in installation. Thousands of architects and engineers are familiar with the basic existence of the technology of photovoltaics, and perhaps a few hundred have direct involvement in designing PV systems. And in practically every suburban shopping area in the United States there is a home-improvement emporium, a tinkerer's candy store, fully capable of stocking photovoltaics right next to the plywood. In short, a vital solar-heating industry exists that will probably undergo a traumatic period of change in 1985–86 owing to the loss of federal tax credits in 1985. As the total price declines, the distribution infrastructure will just take on another product.

Explosion of Innovations in Photovoltaics

When the photovoltaic industry was not an industry and PVs were only a minor product to electrify the occasional satellite, the handful of researchers who even knew of the technology shared bits of new information in quiet discussions that outsiders could barely understand. In our world of excessively specialized knowledge, we have become accustomed to hearing mention of obscure groups who have devoted their lives, or all their spare time, to the minutiae of some extraordinarily narrow field of interest. In Silicon Valley, California, one might hear a scientist bragging about how he figured out a new technique to etch a smoother cut into a semiconductor junction no bigger than a flea's leg. The four people he's bragging to are the only four people on the entire planet who both understand what he's talking about and appreciate the significance of a discovery few people can even see. There was a time when photovoltaic research was like that, and hardly anyone cared.

In 1965 fewer than 100 people were actively involved in various activities related to photovoltaic research. In 1985 probably more than 8000 people worldwide are involved in various aspects of photovoltaic research. That transition, from few to many, has resulted not only in the spread of knowledge but in the rapid proliferation of potential relationships, both technical and social. If only two people know about a particular subject and tell one another what they know, there's nothing else to say about that subject and they can easily exhaust their creative energies about it within a short time. But as the circle widens, the number of potential connections and relationships increases enormously while the body of information thus generated fuels still more connections. The information, whether spoken or written in magazines and technical papers, begins to have a kind of life unto itself. Inevitably, those involved in the research effort begin to perceive long-term patterns and trends that were not visible when the research was just starting. So begins a coevolutionary dialogue among the researchers resulting from the recording of knowledge.

Paralleling the growth of relationships and knowledge related to it, the photovoltaic industry has dramatically risen in value, cultural as well as economic. This is reflected in larger public and private research budgets, new people and institutions entering the business, and a sense that the knowledge is more than mere creative energy—it is translatable to money.

Exponentially, and unpredictably, any growing industry comes to a point in its history where the critical mass of information, relationships, and values coalesces and the industry explodes in a rush of innovation. In such a period, usually lasting only a few years, maybe a decade, it seems as if the industry has no bounds. All innovations seem instantly possible, financing seems available based on a ghost of a business plan jotted on the back of an envelope, and the innovators become heroes whose every utterance could be *it*.

We have probably just witnessed the euphoric rush of innovation in the computer and semiconductor industries between the mid-seventies to early eighties. It happened before and it will probably happen again. Indeed, if some researchers are correct, the next rush in the computer and communications industry will arrive around the turn of the century, when biotechnology merges with electronics to produce memory devices and circuitry that is grown as a new plant is grown. We have also witnessed the dark side of this golden moment—the swindlers and money sharks, the inevitable bankruptcies.

The photovoltaic industry is now displaying all the signs that it is about to enter a period of exploding growth, innovation, and wealth. A sure sign that an industry is maturing in both its technical sophistication and its alignment with the marketplace is a perceptible shift from "pure" scientific research to more market-oriented application research. ARCO Solar began producing single-crystal cells of the most dependable and conservative form in the late seventies. The cells were based on photovoltaic and semiconductor research that had been well established for a few years. In the same period, Solarex began producing similar cells, as did a few other firms. These initial mass-production efforts were based on pure research that dated back to RCA's pioneering work in the late fifties.

These early products were certainly workable—many are now out in the world functioning every day—but they had minor tech-

Photovoltaic Materials and Potentials

Silicon-based:

Single-crystal: Currently a dominant technology. Potential improvements in ingot formation and cutting techniques. Cost may decline due to use of less pure silicon.

Polycrystal: Only slightly less efficient than single-crystal. Cost and production economies are being improved by new ribbon growth techniques and casting technology.

Amorphous: Low efficiency cells already used in consumer products. For exterior applications durability remains a problem, but is being solved. Potential improvements in coating techniques, production technology, substrate materials, and methods of integrating amorphous coatings with building materials will set the stage for widespread use, and much lower costs.

Non silicon-based:

Copper—indium—diselenide: Highest thin-film efficiency—11 percent—has been achieved. Material is sensitive to 67 percent of light spectrum, which is unusually high.

Cadmium telluride: Efficiencies in excess of 13 percent achieved in single-crystal form. Thin-film cells regularly reach 9 to 11 percent efficiency. Material is very promising but expensive.

Copper selenide: Cell efficiency in laboratory conditions has reached 5 to 6 percent. Potential efficiency may be about 10 percent. Advantage of this material is its very low cost.

Copper sulfide: Efficiency as high as 10 to 11 percent but material can be unstable leading to durability problems.

Gallium arsenide: In single-crystal form efficiency can exceed 22 percent. High efficiency may offset the high cost and manufacturing difficulties with this material.

In addition to these materials research is on-going in the use of copper oxides, cadmium selenide and zinc phosphide.

Structures:

Cell junctions: There is research now being done on ways of increasing the efficiency of the barrier layer, or junction, within a cell.

Multi-junction cells: Also known as "cascade" cells these devices involve multiple layers of various materials to allow the widest spectrum of light to be transformed into electricity.

Organic and electro-chemical cells: Wholly new forms of photovoltaics that use an organic compound's receptivity to light, or the reaction of specific chemicals to light, to generate electricity.

nical problems unrelated to the cell functioning. Aluminum frames did not quite fit tightly enough to provide a moisture-proof seal, or the laminated plastic skin separated from the cell surface. As such minor problems were corrected, the cell manufacturers more precisely identified the product weaknesses in terms of the market and environment in which they were to be used. By 1980, both ARCO and Solarex were producing highly dependable products whose production-line and package problems had been solved.

These first ARCO and Solarex products, and those of other companies producing similar modules, became leaders in establishing the market. Now both companies have not only refined their basic product, single- and polycrystalline cells in mass-produced modules, but have begun to introduce amorphous silicon panels based on research they did while concentrating on the sale of their original single-crystal products. The first step, single crystal, had been a conservative move to develop and hold a market, and it set the stage for subsequent developments in both improved versions of the original product and new types of cells.

Researchers at Bell Labs back in the middle fifties were elated to achieve 6 percent efficiency with a simple silicon cell. At that time research into photovoltaics was little more than a laboratory curiosity. Even after the first use of PVs on satellites in the late fifties, research tended to be a single-track effort focused almost entirely on single-crystal silicon and a few exotic variations. Stan Ovshinsky began exploring the potential of amorphous in the early sixties but practically no one believed his theories about amorphous materials until the early seventies, and even then there was considerable doubt.

The single-track effort to develop a highly efficient single-crystal cell split into multiple tracks in the early seventies as a growing number of people became involved in the field and, simultaneously, work in electronic semiconductors yielded a dizzying array of possibilities for new photovoltaics. Ovshinsky's company, Energy Conversion Devices, began to attract serious financial attention in the first years of the decade, and a whole new track, amorphous silicon, emerged. Amorphous was a possibility completely out of left field—it even violated a number of basic principles physicists still argue about. Meanwhile, work in single- and polycrystal silicon was beginning to yield lower cost cells with higher efficiencies. At the same time, feedback from a number of remote-site applications installed in the 1960s was pointing the way to a more durable product and a wide-open market—thousands of remote telecommunications, railroad, gas-pipeline, and pumping sites where utility electricity was out of the question.

In 1975, both private and government-funded research was focused on a hundred interrelated aspects of photovoltaics. While researchers continued to seek more efficient single-crystal silicon—including methods of purifying silicon, producing silicon ingots, cutting ingots to produce wafers, improving production line values, laminating cells into modules, and developing wiring techniques—research was revealing a raft of new possibilities in polycrystal, amorphous, and exotics, such as gallium arsenide cells. The late seventies saw the practical mass production of single crystal at efficiencies in excess of 12 percent, with polycrystal right behind, and all other potentials rapidly gaining. Industry observers such as Paul Maycock, who puts out the industry's most respected newsletter, began to track the various efforts and write about each as if they were watching an ongoing horse race. Given the fact that even a small portion of the world's energy business is a multibillion dollar industry, it was now clear that the horses in this race represented bets that could pay off regardless of whether one held a win, place, or show ticket.

"Pure" research tends to be focused on abstract, even academic, objectives. Much of the early research in photovoltaics was done when researchers could only make wild guesses about the viability of the technology in the context of real-world economic and social realities. As research efforts become linked to products on the market—in the same way production-line research became related to Solarex's products in the late seventies—the complexion of the work changes radically. Instead of being abstract and somewhat distant from the real world, research becomes closely tied to specific objectives—and thus to time frames established by market and economic forces over which researchers have little or no control. Then the race is on, for each step has potentially enormous implications that can be gauged against experience with products already on the market. Current research is thus measured against the performance of single-crystal silicon cells, especially those manufactured by ARCO and Solarex, since they have been on the market longest. When "pure" research dominated the field, it was as if all the horses were being trained by their owners on isolated tracks. Now a number of horses are on the track and running, and there are people in the stands with tickets in their hands.

Mobil Solar Energy Corporation began as a quiet joint venture with Tyco Laboratories in January 1975. The company's first effort involved the development of a square cell grown as a ribbon rather than cut from a round ingot. The firm pioneered a technique known as "edge-defined film-fed growth," which essentially means the pulling of molten crystalline silicon through a precisely shaped die. The ribbon is then sliced by laser into 2 × 4-inch squares, which are, in turn, assembled into 4 × 8-foot panels—the same size as a standard sheet of plywood. The resulting panels, or modules, have been used in a variety of applications—to power streetlights, desalinization plants, and a few houses—and they are now clearly a proven technology with efficiencies in the 9 to 11 percent range.

The first single-crystal cells manufactured by ARCO Solar were round, because they were sliced from round ingots. When these round cells were mounted in a module, even if nested in the tightest possible arrangement, considerable space was left in the inter-

The advantages of square versus round cells. In the background is a standard round cell module; above it is a large panel composed of small square cells. In the foreground are two square cells, one polished without wires, the other completed. The cells were made by Westinghouse Electric Corporation using their dendritic-web ribbon-growing technology.

(Source: Southern California Edison)

stices between the circles. Every square inch that is not covered with silicon is not generating electricity, which means that the entire module's area is not producing electricity. Mobil's ribbon-growth technique results in square cells that totally fill the module's area; furthermore, the entire sawing process with its attendant losses is avoided. Though of lower efficiency compared with ingot-grown cells, ribbon-grown cells offset the difference through the close packing of square cells.

Mobil's more recent development—the new ribbon-pulling process described earlier, in which a nonagon instead of a single ribbon is drawn from molten silicon—effectively increases the efficiency of producing ribbon-grown cells. The crucible and ribbon-pulling machine, which is about the size of a kitchen stove, is approximately the same size and requires the same intermittent monitoring as a single-ribbon machine, but it increases production by almost 900 percent.

Meanwhile, ARCO Solar researchers have not exactly been resting in their efforts to develop ever more efficient and marketable products. In 1984 they introduced a new series of modules using square cells cut from ingots. Except for a tiny square space at the intersection of each square cell, the cells now entirely cover the modules.

The race to fill the module space characterizes both the transition from pure to applied research and the driving competitive forces that propel such seemingly unimportant efforts. The researcher working at Jet Propulsion Lab in 1966 might have been obsessed with increasing efficiency from a single cell on the lab table, and would have considered the density of cell packing in a module a remote concern. But now all companies in the photovoltaic industry are and must be concerned with every aspect of production, manufacture, and installation. Even the choice of module dimensions—ARCO's 12 × 48 inches compared with Mobil's 48 inches wide—both intended to fit standard building construction dimensions—becomes a matter of some concern.

Where the industry's primary concern—and its source of bread and butter through government-financed research projects—was once pure research, it is now increasingly divided into government contracts and proprietary work. Under federal Department of Energy research-grant programs, managed by the Solar Energy Research Institute (SERI), more than 585 research papers were published in fiscal years 1982 and 1983. The scope of the research completed in this one period is staggering. It includes such diverse objectives as the development of a gallium arsenide and silicon stacked cell for use under a concentrator lens—resulting in substantial increases in efficiency—and the development of a fluidized bed reactor to lower the cost of converting silane to silicon. The companies involved in this research range from such corporations as Westinghouse, IBM, and Xerox to consulting firms such as Bechtel, Varian Associates, and Stanford Research Institute. In the late seventies and early eighties, four utilities, seventeen photovoltaic manufacturers, fifty-five corporations of all types and sizes, and fifty-seven universities have been involved in federally financed photovoltaic research. In addition to all these organizations, three California utilities and at least a few dozen private consultants have been involved in various aspects of photovoltaic equipment design and system installation with research implications for the entire industry.

At the time of this writing, it is impossible to predict the level of research funding and the complexion of the research that will occur in fiscal years 1986 through 1988. The Reagan administration has not exactly been fond of photovoltaic research, but a modest budget has been maintained through the administration's first term. Between 1980 and 1984, research has been focused on pure as opposed to applied research, on the assumption that the private sector will be increasingly able to finance applied research. In any case, and despite broadly based federal budget cuts, photovoltaic research will continue under Department of Energy grants.

The multifaceted research program managed by the Solar Energy Research Institute between 1980 and 1984 reflects the ongoing race among many technologies, and the parallel research going on in numerous companies. Research to date also points the way to efforts that will be the focus of subsequent work in the mid to late eighties.

If there is one driving force, one key objective of practically all research into photovoltaic technology, it is the relationship between price and efficiency. Where price is high the efficiency must be high; if the efficiency is low the price per unit of electricity must also be low. A thousand variables are involved in reaching a single alteration in this equation, and the research work supported by SERI plus various efforts going on in private companies are focused on many of these variables.

Most of the research done to date has looked into methods of increasing cell efficiency and lowering production costs. Various methods of producing single- and polycrystalline silicon and of reducing the cost of purifying silicon are aimed at improving the efficiency/cost ratio of technology that is already on the market. In relation to that objective, other work centers on producing low-cost concentrating cells using lenses to increase the amount of sunlight focused on a single cell. Meanwhile, both private firms and SERI are exploring the potentials of amorphous silicon and thin-film gallium arsenide cells. Gallium arsenide, although an exotic substance that is very costly to produce, is unusually receptive to a wide band of lightwaves and is therefore capable of high output—lab cells have achieved 22 percent. Evolving from research in thin-film technology—methods of coating materials with paintlike surfaces that are semiconductive—is ongoing work being done in multi-junction or cascade cells, which achieve higher efficiency by capturing light in successive levels of different materials. On the outer edge of cell technology are liquid-junction cells, which have received relatively little attention but may represent the first step in the merging of "hard" semiconductor technology and "soft" biochemical technology. On the mundane levels, research is also underway into techniques of producing cells and modules to achieve the lowest costs and longest life spans—thirty years is the objective.

As noted, growing silicon crystal ingots from a molten pool results in a cylindrical shape that must be cut into wafers. Ribbon-pulling techniques are a means of growing a shape that is inherently more suitable for photovoltaics. Research efforts have resulted in at least three other methods of producing silicon in sheet form, and thus eliminating the sawing process necessary with solid-ingot production.

As molten silicon is drawn from the crucible, like molten steel, it cools and solidifies. If the crucible is precisely designed with a cooling element in its center and small ridges lying just beneath the surface of the molten silicon, a ribbon can be pulled off the surface of the pool. The cooling element, in combination with a raised-edge stabilizer, causes a thermal barrier to occur within the silicon just as a barrier can exist between levels of hot and cool water in a pond. Consequently, the ribbon is being drawn from a molten section of the pool across a slightly cooler section at a low angle. The technique is called low-angle silicon sheet growth, or LASS. The advantage of this technique is its potential in producing unusually wide sheets of silicon at relatively high speeds. As a result, the amount of high-quality polycrystalline produced per minute is very high in relation to ribbon techniques.

Imagine a pool of water containing a large proportion of dishwashing detergent. Using a piece of straight wire bent into a U shape, dip the wire into the pool and gradually pull it upwards with the U inverted. As the wire emerges from the water a bubble will form between the two wires.

The pool is molten silicon and the wires are graphite rods capable of withstanding the intense heat. The process is called edge-supported pulling. A seed crystal is placed between the two graphite rods before they are dipped into the white-hot silicon. As the rods are gradually withdrawn, a membrane of molten silicon forms between them, gradually solidifying into a solid sheet. As the bubblelike sheet forms—it looks like translucent glowing glass—a polycrystalline structure results. Although the resulting cells are not as efficient as single-crystal cells (13 to 14 percent efficiency compared to 16 to 18 percent), the production costs may be low enough to offset the loss.

A third technique for producing silicon cells involves a process that seems oddly simple: a cooled, rapidly spinning disk becomes the platform for the pouring of molten silicon. As the liquid silicon hits the center of the disk, centrifugal force causes it to spread evenly outwards from the center. The result is a thin sheet of polycrystalline silicon.

Further exploration into methods of silicon-cell production will no doubt be heavily influenced by market forces yet to be defined. As the industry grows, specific technologies may become increasingly tied to particular markets and applications. Notably, amorphous silicon thin-film cells have already become identified with a wide range of consumer products and will probably be used in automobiles within the next five to ten years. In those applications, the relatively low efficiency of amorphous materials is offset not only by the low cost of amorphous cells, but by the low power requirements of their applications—recharging batteries in clocks, radios, televisions, watches, calculators, computers, and automobiles.

Amorphous research begun by RCA in the early seventies, and paralleled by the research of Energy Conversion Devices in the late sixties and early seventies, resulted in the first patents being issued in 1973–74. RCA continued its research into amorphous technology through the 1970s and early eighties until it found itself losing money on a number of unrelated new ventures and sold the amorphous venture to Solarex. In 1983 and 1984, Solarex began further development work on the foundation RCA had laid. The firm's efforts paralleled an industrywide effort to develop and market amorphous products, efforts that are accelerating in direct response to intense Japanese, and to a lesser extent European, research into amorphous cells.

Amorphous materials are inherently disordered; they are not produced with crystalline lattices of diamond form as is crystalline or polycrystalline silicon. Instead, the atomic structure is chaotic. While the efficiency is lower than single-crystal or polycrystalline silicon or gallium arsenide cells, amorphous materials require between a hundredth and a five-hundredth of the material used in crystalline cells. Furthermore, the silicon used in a typical amorphous cell can be deposited from silane gas directly onto a substrate material, such as stainless steel. Silane-gas production is a primary step in purifying silicon, so instead of the gas becoming a solid and then the solid being remelted and formed into ingots or ribbons, it can be deposited directly. Obviously, this sidesteps a series of processes required in crystalline-silicon production—ingot and ribbon forming, sawing, surface treating of a solid cell—and as a result is inherently more economical. Although at 6 to 8 percent amorphous cells are less efficient than the others, the savings in production costs more than offsets the loss.

Practically all major photovoltaic firms are now involved in various aspects of development work on amorphous cells. ARCO Solar recently introduced an amorphous panel, Solarex continues to develop amorphous technology under a cloak of secrecy, and at least a dozen other U.S. firms are actively working on amorphous materials, production techniques, and advanced concepts. There is widespread agreement within the industry that amorphous will become a market leader within four to eight years.

Cascade cells do not represent an enormous market potential right around the corner but they do represent the possibility of a highly efficient and low-cost cell. Each layer of a cascade cell is very precisely composed to capture a specific wavelength within the solar spectrum. In essence a cascade cell is analogous to a sequence of increasingly finer screens. The top screen has large holes, the next smaller holes, the next still smaller holes, while the bottom screen is almost solid. The successive layers allow some photons to pass through while others are "caught" and transformed into electricity.

The architecture of a cascade cell, the thickness and composition of its sandwiched layers, is unusually critical and the source of production difficulties. Work has barely begun on cascade cells, but much of the research completed to date indicates that the concept is clearly feasible but not easy to realize.

The beauty of the cascade concept is the ability to transform an extraordinarily high proportion of sunlight. In a sense one might say it responds to all the colors. While the theoretical efficiency is close to 35 percent, the actual efficiency of production cells might be in the 28 to 32 percent range. Amorphous materials and the various deposition techniques developed to lay silicon down in very thin coatings have set the stage for cascade cells. The research now being done is focused on methods of laying down many layers atop one another without damaging the layers beneath in the process—each layer is about 100 angstroms thick.

Clearly the research that began as an idle curiosity in the mid-fifties has exploded into a broad range of directions, each representing questions, and answers, that no one could have imagined a mere fifteen years ago. Earlier research and development efforts concentrated on the mechanics of cell construction and module manufacture, but the rapidly expanding research into amorphous materials now increasingly involves the development of thin coatings upon glass or steel. What was a process of assembling diverse pieces of metal, plastic, glass, and silicon is becoming a process of applying a single sequence of coatings on one material.

If one word characterizes current photovoltaic research it is portentous. The combination of intrinsically simple production methods and commonplace materials suggests that electricity generating is about to become simpler than ever before.

The Fickleness of Federal Photovoltaic Policy

The federal government of the United States, as well as the national governments of other countries with photovoltaic industries, has been the industry's first customer and investor of last resort. The rate of the industry's development has been due in part to assistance from federal and some state governments in the form of tax credits and research grants. It has been, and still is, assumed that with this modest assistance the price of photovoltaics would drop and a substantial industry would be born. In essence, the government becomes a primary force in instigating the formation and development of a whole series of economic linkages. Unfortunately, and in contrast with the governments of other nations, notably Japan, the U.S. government has been somewhat fickle in its support of the photovoltaic industry. Support has wavered repeatedly and it now wanes under a presidential administration that seems incapable of developing any sensible energy policy consistent with utility, consumer, environmental, financial, and technological realities.

Between 1958 and 1975, the government indirectly sponsored the industry by purchasing photovoltaics for satellites under various National Aeronautics and Space Administration programs. This resulted in much of the basic research that led to the development of more widely commercial photovoltaic products in the mid-seventies. Since 1975, research under the Department of Energy, primarily through the Solar Energy Research Institute, has both broadened our knowledge and assisted in the formation of numerous corporations. In partnership with many of those corporations, SERI research has further resulted in a drastic decline in price, by a factor of 20, and a 100 percent increase in average cell efficiency. Photovoltaics are now far more durable, lasting ten times longer than those made in the early seventies and encased in modules of sophisticated yet simple design. And production costs are now about one-quarter to one-fifth what they were in 1975. But the price of photovoltaics is still not quite low enough to penetrate major utility markets without tax credits. It is very close in some

Utility Options, 1985–2000

Conservation: Involves simple technical fixes to existing structures and meets with little political opposition. Yields a decrease in consumption of between 10 and 50 percent.

Solarization: Minor alterations to existing structures to increase solar heat gain. Utilities can assist in the sale and installation of technology.

Cogeneration: Usually a diesel-electric generating system located in a building or complex of buildings. The hot water from the diesel engine is used for building heat. Can be very efficient.

Biomass: Wood and agricultural waste burned in a boiler to generate steam that drives turbines/generators. Feasible and already proven in many areas of the country.

Waste: Burning of garbage or other waste to generate steam and drive turbines/generators. Feasible but involves some environmental problems due to potentially toxic stack emissions.

Hydroelectric, large: Dam holds back water; water is piped to turbines driving generators. Feasible, but suitable sites are rare and cost is high. Serious political problems due to cost and adverse environmental impact.

Hydroelectric, small: Dam or small catch basin with pipe to small turbine/generator. Highly feasible; now being built in many areas. Output relatively low, but involves few political, financial, or environmental problems.

Wind: Single or clustered windmills. Applicable in many windy areas of the country. Technically simple and proven technology is now available and cost-competitive.

Geothermal: Involves tapping underground heat sources, generating steam to drive turbines/generators. Feasible but limited to certain geothermally active areas of the U.S. Not widely applicable.

Oil or natural gas: Fuel burned in boilers; steam to turbines driving generators. Well-established technology. Economy of scale requires large plants that are costly and time consuming to build. Fuel price problematical.

Coal: Fuel burned in boilers; steam to turbines driving generators. Most established technology. Fuel low in cost and available in long term but coal mining and stack emissions entail serious problems.

Nuclear: Uranium chain reaction heats water, steam to turbines driving generators. Owing to financial and political problems, not an option in most cases.

Solar-thermal, central tower: Mirrors focus sunlight on central tower containing heat-transfer medium; steam to turbines/generators. Feasible, almost cost-competitive. Applicable primarily in Sunbelt.

Solar-thermal, small trackers: Mirrors generate heat/steam for turbines/generators. Feasible and cost-competitive now. Applicable primarily in Sunbelt.

Photovoltaics, large-scale: Tracking photovoltaic panels in fields. Now proven and possible with very short construction times. Not quite economically competitive, but will be widely applicable as price declines.

Photovoltaics, cogeneration: Tracking/concentrating PV systems generating electricity and hot water. Now proven but still too expensive. As price declines, will be widely applicable to buildings.

Photovoltaics, rooftop: Existing modules installed on home and commercial buildings. Utility could act as distributor/installer. Highly feasible; will soon be cost-competitive in much of the U.S.

Ocean-temperature gradient: Water column located offshore; turbines driven by upwelling water currents. Probably feasible but no large-scale facilities have been built yet. Use as yet unpredictable.

Fuel cells: Analogous to diesel-electric cogeneration but fuel (natural gas, oil, etc.) is chemically "burned," producing electricity directly and some hot water. Feasible but only minimally used so far.

---

areas of the country, but not quite there.

Under the administration of President Jimmy Carter, the photovoltaic industry gained a solid foothold. Department of Energy research into all forms of solar energy, including photovoltaics, was increased dramatically. In the same period, planning and budgeting in photovoltaic research was occurring in France, Italy, Japan, West Germany, Belgium, Australia, China, England, Canada, India, Mexico, Brazil, Netherlands, Sweden, Spain, and the Soviet Union. While at the time of this writing research and development funding in the United States exceeds that of any other country, both Japan and some European nations are steadily closing the gap.

Under the administration of Ronald Reagan, photovoltaic research was cut back substantially. Private firms had been increasing their research and development budgets anyway, so their efforts have, to some extent, made up for the loss. But this investment is directly tied to product sales that are, in many cases, directly related to the tax-credit programs on the state and federal levels. In essence the tax credits, particularly on the federal level, encourage sales and therefore higher production volumes. Higher volume sales and income result in further production economies and sufficient funds to engage in increasingly proprietary and competitive research. Now the tax credit, due to expire in December of 1985, is threatened. The Reagan administration does not advocate continuing the credit program.

Historically there are three forms of direct subsidy and one form of indirect subsidy. The U.S. government, with respect to the entire photovoltaics and renewable industry, has favored the industry with tax credits, research and development funding, and purchase assistance when the technology is used on government buildings—two forms of direct subsidy and one of indirect subsidy. Indirect subsidy usually takes the form of policies adopted by federal agencies to encourage use of the new technology when and where possible. While favorable policies can result in federal agencies making major purchases of photovoltaic products, the validating effects of such policies are perhaps more important.

Those within the photovoltaic and solar industries generally feel that subsidies of any kind are an unfortunate fact of life. Regardless of whether we choose to believe in free-market economics, and attempt to enact those beliefs in government policies, practically all governments now aware of photovoltaics and their potential are increasing their research budgets and coordinating their foreign policies with photovoltaic development. If we, as a nation, choose to ignore this fact, we risk losing the lead in photovoltaic development to the Japanese and Europeans—even though we initiated the development of the technology.

However, since 1918 practically all other energy sources—coal, oil, nuclear, and hydroelectric—have received substantially greater subsidies. The federal government has directly and indirectly subsidized conventional energy sources to the tune of $125 to $300 billion—$1.9 to 4.5 billion annually for sixty-seven years. And those figures do not include a staggering range of "other" costs, such as acid rain and air pollution, and the cost of decommissioning and dealing with exhausted nuclear power plants. The latter cost may, over the next thirty years, amount to over $100 billion.

Clearly, the most painful and frustrating aspect of the subsidy issue is the inequitable arrangement that is now in force. Billions of dollars are committed to subsidizing other forms of energy while the solar industry, with minimal subsidies or none at all, is expected to compete. Furthermore, the solar industry, most notably photovoltaics, will eliminate many of the "other" costs that have resulted from intensive development of practically all other sources. But even the Carter administration, which was generally supportive of solar, chose to ignore the blatant imbalance in energy-industry subsidies and the increasingly costly implications of further developing conventional sources of energy. Typically, the Carter administration, under intense lobbying from the oil industry, originated the synfuels program aimed at developing non-imported sources of oil from various domestic coal reserves.

Clarity, where competing options are concerned, rarely prevails. Policy making in Washington, D.C., tends to be dominated equally by special interest groups and a rational perception of the facts. Those who scream loudest and longest often receive the federal largesse. Inevitably, this results in the furtherance of policies and subsidies that favor major industries regardless of the larger and longer term implications of such assistance. This understandable dynamic between industry and lawmakers is no doubt reinforced by the sheer complexity of the information involved and the often subjective nature of that information. Any special interest

The Sacramento Municipal Utility District's 1-megawatt photovoltaic generating facility. This photograph was taken in the morning in June of 1984, just after completion of phase one. The panels are tilted to catch the morning sun. In the background is the Rancho Seco nuclear power plant. The two towers exhaust steam—waste heat—and the round building shaped like a coffee can is the reactor. When complete, the PV plant will supply about one-ninth of the nuclear plant's output. The entire site is known by employees as "the Ranch."

(Source: Sacramento Municipal Utility District)

group, on any side of any issue, can muster copious facts to bolster any argument.

Creating the barrage of papers, letters, and reports that support one position or another represents a cottage industry in technical analysis—in the manufacture of ammunition. But beneath the crossfire of technical minutiae lie certain elemental facts that are simply inescapable. Unfortunately, these facts almost always get lost in presentations of complex issues supported by copious numbers. It almost seems as if intrinsic values are rendered totally meaningless in the face of statistics.

Photovoltaics, and most renewable technologies, are intrinsically more efficient than their conventional counterparts. It does not take any complex analysis to perceive this central fact; one simply has to look at the technology and what it does. A mere photograph of the Rancho Seco nuclear power plant that shows the photovoltaic plant right next door speaks volumes about the inherent differences between the two technologies. As billowing clouds pour forth from the nuclear plant's cooling towers, owing to the excessive *waste* heat nuclear plants generate, the photovoltaic plant silently generates electricity. Around the nuclear plant are dozens of supporting structures. Next door, the photovoltaic facility has only one small building containing power-conditioning and monitoring equipment: it has no central control facility, no elaborate control systems, no endless modifications, and only a fraction of the nuclear plant's support technology. In short, the photovoltaic facility has practically no moving parts, except the panels that slowly track the sun, and produces no excess heat and no air or water pollution of any kind.

It is true that the conventional definition of efficiency only includes the immediate generation of electricity, not all the costs and inefficiencies of the entire process, and on that basis, photovoltaics are less efficient than conventional sources. But when the obvious advantages of the technology are included and compared to conventional sources with *all* their costs included, the story is quite different. Of course, this means that those supporting conventional technologies would have to acknowledge and account for the true costs, which up to now they have been notably reticent to do.

Aside from the complex issues of efficiency and subsidy inequities, photovoltaics dovetail with the objectives of practically every cabinet-level agency in the federal government, not to mention their state and local counterparts. Yet as the Grace Commission discovered in the process of studying the federal government, the left hand of the bureaucracy hasn't the remotest idea what the right hand is doing. Furthermore, one agency is often so busy building its own empire it does not have any interest in what another agency might be doing. Nevertheless, if a coordinated federal policy existed it might have a profound effect on the government itself as well as the photovoltaic industry.

As noted earlier, at this writing the solar tax credit is due to expire in December of 1985 and its possible extension is uncertain. Photovoltaic research budgets will probably be continued under the management of the Solar Energy Research Institute, but at a modest level. If the tax credit is not extended it is practically inevitable that Japan's market share, worldwide, will increase and the United States dominance of an industry we founded would diminish. But what if the tax credit were extended as part of a coordinated policy?

A possibility would be to extend the tax credit five more years, to 1990, with each year's credit decreasing to parallel dropping photovoltaic costs. Simultaneously, research grants could be increased modestly, focusing on pure research *and* applications research and emphasizing university work rather than work in private firms. And in connection with these two steps, each affected federal agency could initiate PV-purchase programs.

The departments of Labor and Commerce are those most concerned with fostering economic development. The photovoltaic industry's potential in the United States, in gross income and job potential, is probably greater than any other industry now on the horizon. Undoubtedly, utilities, if they became heavily committed to PVs, would absorb many of the potential jobs, but thousands of other opportunities would be created in the sales, marketing, manufacture, and installation of PV systems. Exporting U.S. made photovoltaics would contribute to reductions in the balance-of-trade deficit. And given the existence of many areas in the United States with severe structural unemployment, and often lower living costs compared with urban areas, it is conceivable that our labor costs in some regions could be more competitive with those for foreign labor.

In advocating PV development, the Department of Energy

would be assisting the development of an industry that would not exacerbate the already horrendous environmental and financial problems of coal and nuclear power; nor would it increase our dependence on foreign oil. A number of utilities in the United States are struggling with the financial problems of nuclear power. In many cases they must increase electric rates dramatically to cover the high costs of nuclear plants about to come on-line. Although the conditions vary from place to place, it is conceivable that a strong Department of Energy policy favoring utility development of photovoltaic systems—on any scale—would result in the development of a lower cost source of electricity that might offset the high costs of existing nuclear plants. In other cases, utility development of PVs, with DOE support, might result in the revitalization of utilities—financially, technologically, and socially.

The Department of State, meanwhile, could integrate photovoltaic development with various foreign aid programs in an effort to create viable local economies not reliant upon endless U.S. aid. Typically, the development of photovoltaic manufacturing plants and related technology in Central American countries would result in a substantial increase in local autonomy, an improvement in medical care, increased access to cultural events and news via television, and a general increase in the overall quality of life. Certainly the value of such action would be profound, and far more lasting than covert military actions, which only address the symptoms, not the causes, of social unrest. Indeed, all the elements—photovoltaics, solar hot-water heating, wood-heating and small hydro systems, high-productivity organic farming, and a wide variety of small-scale industrial strategies—are proven and available ways of initiating a dramatic revitalization of local village life. Economic and social change in the form of solar technology and concepts typically involves both cooperative *and* competitive modes of economic action. It can cut neatly through all abstract political theorizing and result in the growth of local self-reliance with a measure of free enterprise.

Turning now to the Department of the Interior, including the National Park Service and agencies managing various federal lands, it is possible to visualize these agencies initiating the development of photovoltaic-powered facilities in the park- and wildlands they administer. To some extent they have already initiated such an effort by developing PV-powered national park facilities and forestry lookout towers and totally converting an Arizona Indian village into a fully photovoltaic-powered town. Expanding these pioneering programs could, in many instances, result in lower electricity costs for parkland facilities that are now often reliant on diesel generators or vulnerable utility lines. Moreover, in some national parks, notably Yellowstone and Yosemite, transportation is a serious problem. Development of photovoltaic-powered vehicles—small buses or light rail systems—would not only result in less noise and pollution, it would serve as well to demonstrate minimal-impact public transportation.

Innumerable uses of photovoltaic technology present themselves where the Department of Defense is concerned. Remote generating facilities are perhaps the most notable possibility. Photovoltaic and hot-water cogenerating systems on truck trailers are quite feasible and would allow military activities to be sustained regardless of fuel availability—and PV systems would be silent. Dozens of small military vehicles and portable facilities could be PV powered—radar sets, radio systems, aircraft service trucks, portable mess kitchens, portable toilet facilities. Lockheed Aircraft is now constructing a photovoltaic-powered airplane that will be capable of staying aloft to take photographs almost indefinitely.

Perhaps the single largest military option with the greatest impact would be the development of photovoltaic power for military bases and large Navy ships. Military bases almost totally reliant upon solar energy would become self-sustaining and far more difficult to disrupt than conventionally powered bases in the event of war. Navy ships, whether combat or supply oriented, commonly consume a substantial portion of their fuel in generating electricity for on-board use. They also have large expanses of superstructure—areas where photovoltaic panels could easily be integrated into the surface. The result would be an additional source of electricity that could cut fossil-fuel consumption and extend the ship's range while simultaneously providing an emergency source of ample electricity should the ship become disabled at sea. On smaller ships, the power generated might be sufficient to provide an emergency source of motive power.

As this survey shows, government policies and purchase programs could yield substantial opportunities for the development of photovoltaic technology. Any one, two, or three of the potentials described would no doubt unleash a raft of others as yet unimagined. And the scale of government purchases in most of these areas would be so large that a few major orders would result in noticeable production economies. At the very least, the adoption of a federal policy favorable to photovoltaic development would enable the United States to retain the lead in producing technology developed here.

One real tragedy underlies the lack of a consistent and favorable U.S. government policy towards renewables in general and photovoltaics in particular. That is the inability of the government, and of many corporations, to perceive the relationship between our loss of industrial competitive strength and our energy-guzzling habits. No other country's citizens must work for so many hours to pay their energy costs. To the extent that high U.S. energy costs themselves are embodied in the products and services we market to the world, we are less competitive than other countries. So, while the government, and critics in the media, regularly cite our "high labor costs" as the primary explanation for why U.S. jobs are moving overseas, no one attempts to link those high costs with the various underlying costs, in which energy is a major contributing factor. Instead, we have a presidential administration that equates *more* energy use with a healthy economy, as if the United States lived in an economic vacuum. This situation is simply ignorance on a grand scale.

Although it may be too early for certainty, it is highly probable that a sequence of little noticed events in the past five years has closed off all other options for new and expanded electrical-generation capacity—small-scale fossil-fueled cogeneration plants and all renewable technologies may be our only option in the 1990s. The rate of growth necessary to justify large-scale coal or nuclear power plants just isn't there. Small-scale power plants have already gained a substantial foothold in the utility industry. Furthermore, photovoltaics are too close to becoming competitive in too many regions for any U.S. utility to assume that PVs will not be a major new competitive force—a threat to their dominance if they do nothing to counter or include PV technology in their strategies. And the utility industry's generally lackluster financial performance, coupled with nuclear power problems, effectively precludes any large-scale private-sector financial moves. In short, while the federal government debates energy on a piecemeal basis, the real choices may have already been made in the marketplace.

SUNCELL

3: Price Line

Markets Expand as Photovoltaic Prices Decline

While draining a pond one gradually perceives what was out of sight below the water line. Rocks, plants, and shorelines emerge as the area of water shrinks, conforming to the pond's continually changing perimeter.

As the price of photovoltaics declines, the industry itself changes shape in response to the new landscape of markets and opportunities. At this writing, the price line has just begun to reveal a diversity of markets and an enticing array of wholly new possibilities. When the price of photovoltaics-generated electricity was eight dollars a watt, the tip of a single market emerged. At four dollars, the tip has broadened to 500 times its previous size. At each level existing companies develop new products and marketing strategies, and new companies are formed to address specific markets.

A new and unprecedented product often responds to a wide range of variables, with price only one of many considerations. One cannot really identify those variables, or predict how the customer might value the new technology, until the product is out there performing. Obviously, the value of photovoltaics to the space program was simply immeasurable in the usual terms of price, since photovoltaics were effectively the only options. Small nuclear power generators were explored as sources of satellite power but found to be too heavy and expensive.

Out in the middle of the New Mexico desert, four pipes come out of the ground, make a loop, and go right back in again. At the top of the loops, which stand amid the sagebrush like giant hairpins stuck in the sand, are monitors measuring the temperature of gas within the pipes. In the Idaho wilderness, atop a 9000-foot mountain, is a steel tower carrying two large microwave dishes that look like ears listening to the sounds of the plains below. Only a narrow dirt road, impassable in the winter, ties the tower to the civilized world. In northern Oregon, someone makes a phone call to New York; the caller's voice and thousands of others pass through those microwave ears. Out on the high plains of Montana,

Price Line

Price goes down, markets open up:

single-crystal and polycrystal silicon 1984:
to manufacture: $7 to $9 per peak watt

installed cost, with state and federal credits:
as low as $4 to $5 per watt

amorphous silicon:
to manufacture: $2 to $3 per watt

At $10 to $30 per watt installed cost:

Remote microwave stations
Some remote pipeline and railroad applications
Government-sponsored demonstration projects
Some consumer products applications

At $5 to $6 per watt installed:

Irrigation in remote areas
Mountain cabins and recreation vehicles and boats
Villages with no or little electricity now
Pipeline monitoring and railroad equipment

At $2 to $3 per watt installed:

New utility power plants plugged into grid
Houses and farms far from utility grid
Areas where electricity is already expensive
Areas dependent on diesel generators
Homes and commercial buildings in some areas of United States
General use in much of less developed world

At $.50 to $1 per watt installed:

Widely applicable to houses almost everywhere
Consumer product market
Utility-scale plants almost anywhere

At $.30 to $.50 per watt installed:

Competitive with electricity from any source anywhere on Earth

---

along a single track of the Burlington Northern railroad, stands a small silver box with wires connected to the rails. A passing train triggers small relays within the box and a signal turns red, warning any other train from getting too close to the one just passed.

These technological devices in three remote places require relatively small amounts of electricity, hardly enough to justify the expense of building a power line. Traditionally, the only alternatives would be batteries or remote-site generators requiring diesel fuel—both troublesome options and costly to maintain. But like satellites quietly spinning about Earth, these remote devices are anonymous machines that perform critical functions with no one even within earshot. They need simple, trouble-free power sources—photovoltaics.

Indeed, satellites powered by photovoltaics allow practically all our satellite-based telecommunications systems to function, and now a growing number of microwave telephone repeating stations are also powered by the sun. Many of our long-distance phone conversations are currently solar powered.

In remote applications dependability and low maintenance are the cost factors of most importance; price is less significant. Solarex and ARCO Solar, and increasingly Mobil Solar, have developed this market with photovoltaic modules, and whole systems, that allow such remote facilities to operate reliably almost regardless of environmental conditions. At first only the most remote sites, and thus the most expensive to maintain, received photovoltaic power. Now, as the price of PVs comes down, photovoltaics are increasingly replacing power sources in somewhat less remote sites.

A second major market emerged unexpectedly out of nowhere. Thousands of people who had moved to the backwoods corners of the United States in the late sixties and early seventies found themselves in the middle of the wilderness with only kerosene or gas light. For a few years the dim glow of flame was adequate, but increasingly these settlers wanted to expand their activities, perhaps to operate a small cottage industry, and electricity became necessary. Power lines were often out of the question: at prices like $12,000 a mile a few residents living on meager incomes could hardly support such a project. By the late seventies photovoltaic modules at $400 to $600 were available, and many of the cottage industries were based on agricultural enterprises that generated substantial sums of tax-free cash—assuming the growers weren't caught. Although the photovoltaic industry is somewhat reticent to openly admit it, this source of business was a very welcome new market. It is now estimated by various industry observers that between 5,000 and 10,000 houses are now electrified with PV systems of one to ten modules. Although many observers and critics tend to dismiss this market, given its high proportion of illicit cash, the market is by no means confined to hemp growers and does represent a major entry into the home-power market.

The backwoods year-round resident with a photovoltaic power system of modest proportions has pioneered the use of PVs for vacation cabins. In many regions of the United States, Canada, and Mexico, people with medium or high incomes own small vacation cabins that are either far from power lines, and thus use diesel generators, or are susceptible to constant power outages owing to the vulnerability of power lines to wilderness conditions—wind, snow, and ice. Photovoltaic manufacturers are steadily penetrating this market. However, unlike backwoods residences, which had no electricity at all, most vacation cabins have an electrical source and the owners tend to look upon home improvements to their vacation homes as a low priority. As a result, this market may be more price-sensitive than that composed of people who live in remote cabins year round.

The market dynamics of remote-site installations are centered around the promise of reliable, quietly generated electricity. Backwoods residents welcomed the possibility of *any* electricity not requiring complex technology that made noise, required endless maintenance, and tied them to a source of fuel. For both the markets described, price, although hardly irrelevant, was and is secondary to the capability of the technology. For example, a resident of a high alpine area who had had one too many long winters with kerosene light would almost certainly opt for a photovoltaic module and a small lighting system regardless of the fact that the cost,

Photovoltaic Markets

Market segments, 1981	Percentages
Remote communications	48 %
Consumer products, RVs, boats, cars	23
Rural electrification	12
Water pumping	12
Cathodic protection (pipelines)	10

Projected market segments, 2000	Percentages
Grid-tied/stand-alone systems	48 %
Rural electrification	17
Water pumping	11
Remote communications	11
Consumer products, RVs, boats, cars	8
Cathodic protection	5

(Source: Mobil Solar Energy Corp.)

$500, bought nothing more than two small bulbs, a battery, some wiring, and a single module. That consumer would probably buy it even if the price was $800. Someone living in such conditions is, almost literally, a captive market.

Within the photovoltaics industry, the lesson of the backwoods residents suggested some things about the world at large, particularly the Third World. U.S. corporations are not exactly falling all over themselves to meet the market demands of Third World countries with low per capita income levels. As often as not, most U.S. companies look upon such markets as a liability, perhaps even a nuisance. However, depending on whose estimate one believes, somewhere between 60 and 75 percent of the world's population has little or no access to electricity. And many of those that do have access to, say, a central diesel generator coupled to a village-scale grid of light wiring on telephone poles, and even many of those with access to larger regional systems, do not regard electricity as a dependable source of energy. Power levels may fluctuate regularly in such systems and total blackouts are commonplace. In these circumstances even a single photovoltaic panel could represent a breakthrough of enormous meaning—and value.

Practically all U.S., Japanese, and European photovoltaic firms are watching developments in the Third World very closely. A few companies are beginning to make major strides in entering the non-industrialized markets. Notably, Spire Corporation, which does not market photovoltaics but the machines to make them, has sold a number of photovoltaic-manufacturing facilities to major countries in Asia, South America, and the Middle East. Although the price and technological dynamics of this market are so complex as to almost defy description, it is generally true that market entry is happening through government aid—local government as well as outside agencies such as the World Bank—and through local or regional economic development programs. Now, this market is being developed almost entirely with single-crystal and polycrystalline cells. The tantalizing objective is amorphous silicon cells at low prices. There is one word to characterize the worldwide market for cheap amorphous PVs: *enormous*.

There is another huge potential market, one most Americans know intimately. Thousands of consumer and industrial products are made every year in production runs that often measure in the tens of millions. A sizable chunk of this output involves small devices that require a source of electricity to operate—an extension cord or batteries or both. For example, many small calculators need batteries, exhaustable or rechargeable, and cords. The cords are often larger than the objects they are powering, a fact that echoes the transition from 110 volt ac power at an outlet to the trickle of electricity the device requires. Batteries, even rechargeable batteries, are expensive and a nuisance to replace. And in many products the amount of power required is so small, given the efficiencies of tiny integrated circuits, that even using batteries seems like employing nuclear power to light a chicken coop. Predictably, the Japanese, who produce hundreds of millions of electronic consumer products, have pioneered the use of PVs on calculators, watches, portable speakers, microphones, radios, televisions, and now car-battery chargers. In all these devices what is needed is a trickle, not a torrent, of electricity.

In 1984 practically all the world's production of amorphous cells, more than 6.5 megawatts, was in the form of cells placed in Japanese products—about 95 million calculators, 10 million watches, and thousands of other products. In such applications the

A small outdoor light designed to be totally independent of external connections. Conventional outdoor lighting usually requires the installation of an underground conduit, which can be very costly if the light is required some distance from a building.

(Source: Balance of System Specialists)

A totally self-contained exterior lighting system, utilizing a PV panel to recharge the battery pack automatically. The whole package can be installed and practically forgotten until the batteries require replacement in three to six years. Such a system is useful for industrial installations that require outdoor lights for nighttime operations and security. Often, sites requiring light do not coincide with the location of outlets or underground conduits.

efficiency of amorphous cells, around 5-7 percent, is almost meaningless, since the cells are small and add little to the product's cost
while often eliminating batteries both as a cost and a design problem. Japanese photovoltaic companies, primarily Fuji and Sanyo,
are using the consumer market as a means of generating an amorphous market, research, and financial base from which they can
launch into larger applications on homes and other buildings.

U.S. companies, notably Energy Conversion Devices in a joint
venture with Japan's Sharp Electronics, have begun to enter the
market for consumer products with amorphous cells incorporated
into their design. And other companies within the United States
have developed and marketed versions of their regular photovoltaic
modules for other consumer applications—boats, recreational vehicles, and most recently golf carts. Traditionally these applications
have involved battery recharging, which usually means running a
portable generator—the boat or RV's engine—or plugging the cart
into a wall socket. PV systems eliminate the annoyance of constantly recharging batteries. In the case of RV owners, as with the
wilderness dwellers described earlier, price is far less important
than the simplicity and convenience of a battery that is quietly
charged every day while the owner gives it little or no thought.

While the consumer-product market is growing, the potential
market for the wide range of industrial and larger products about
to include photovoltaic power remains unfathomable. These potentials are so numerous it would take a page to list them, but without
a doubt the largest involves automotive transportation. Every
major automobile manufacturer is studying methods of installing
photovoltaics, probably amorphous, into car, truck, and bus roofs.
A relatively small panel, one or two square feet in size, would provide a trickle charge to the battery and reduce the load on the alternator, thus reducing fuel consumption and increasing battery life.

The marketing of photovoltaic cells will increasingly cause a
ripple effect in related industries. Makers of small batteries will
lose as a growing percentage of small consumer products become
PV powered. Large automotive-battery producers may lose sales
too if PV use on cars results in longer battery life. On the other
hand, however, they will also gain as more batteries are sold for
home electrical storage in PV systems. The most vulnerable are
companies now producing small portable generators. Photovoltaics
are likely to replace almost the entire market for such machines.

The Phenomenal Growth of Small-Scale Power Systems

While the media might have been focusing on the major issues, such as the fate of nuclear energy, the utility industry has been quietly moving towards small-scale power systems since the mid-1970s. In 1985 104 utilities in the United States are either researching or developing wind energy systems; Wisconsin Power and Light is in the wind turbine business as a manufacturer. The following summarizes the trends:

Pacific Gas & Electric Company, San Francisco, California: In 1983 PG & E's peak load demand was 15,156 megawatts. In other words that is the amount of power the company had to generate to meet demand on the hottest afternoon of the year.

In 1984 PG & E operated only 684 megawatts of small-scale power plants. Some of this output came from renewable sources, some from non-renewable such as diesel-fueled cogeneration plants.

By 1985 PG & E had an additional 2,198 megawatts of small-scale generating plants under construction, and 2,155 megawatts in the planning stages.

If PG & E builds all planned facilities, it will receive about a third of its 1983 peak load demand from small-scale sources by the middle of the next decade. Much of this electricity will be generated by wind farms, some from photovoltaic facilities.

Southern California Edison, Los Angeles, California: SCE has been a pioneer in small-scale system development. It now receives power from three solar-thermal facilities, a number of photovoltaic facilities of all sizes, various small-scale geothermal projects, and a variety of other small-scale plants.

If all existing, planned, and proposed small-scale systems are built, SCE could receive over a third of its peak load capacity from small-scale sources by the middle of the next decade.

On the national scale: Since the mid-1970s, but particularly in the early 1980s, small-scale power plant construction has expanded at a very rapid rate. If all plants scheduled are operating in 1986, approximately 14,000 megawatts—the equivalent of 10 to 18 conventional nuclear or coal power plants—will be on-line.

The growth by type of facility:

Cogeneration: The conventional form of cogenerating power system involves an internal combustion engine—diesel, gas—driving a generator with the engine's waste heat being piped off for use as hot water within a building or factory. Typically, a cogenerator is installed in a single building or complex of buildings. It provides electricity and hot water with surplus electricity sold back to the utility.

In 1975 practically no cogeneration systems were being designed or built. By 1980 319 megawatts were in planning stages. By 1985 9,000 megawatts are operating or planned.

Biomass: This energy source, usually agricultural waste or forest slash, was practically ignored in 1975. Ten years later 1,786 megawatts is being generated, or soon will be, by biomass power plants.

Small-Scale Hydro: Another ignored energy source. It has grown from 59 megawatts output in 1980 to over 929 megawatts in 1985. Advocates suggest that the potential may be at least ten times current output.

Wind Power: There were fewer than 100 machines in use for utility production in 1980, now there are over 9,000. The industry went from 76 to over 800 megawatts in only five years. Most of this output is concentrated around a few sites in California.

Geothermal: In 1980 a mere 76 megawatts were generated. If current projects are completed as planned, over 500 megawatts will be generated from the Earth's heat by 1986.

Waste: Garbage burns, and both European and Japanese garbage burning plants have proven the feasibility of the technology with minimal environmental impacts. In the U.S. output has grown from 1 megawatt in 1980 to 295 megawatts in 1985.

Solar thermal and photovoltaic: Zero output on the utility scale in 1980. Now approximately 100 megawatts either operating or planned in 1985.

Conclusion: There is little doubt that small-scale power generation—renewable and non-renewable—has gained a solid foothold in the utility industry. Behind this remarkable growth are some elementary financial facts. If the same output—approximately 14,000 megawatts—were to have been generated by conventional means, it would have required the construction of 10 to 18 facilities at $2 to $5 billion each. That translates to a commitment of $20 to $90 billion tied up in construction for at least 4, and at most 10, years. And during that time no electricity would be produced.

With photovoltaic products finding their way into the marketplace, prices are now down to the point where the technology is both cheap enough and dependable enough to be considered as back-up or sole electricity source for millions of civic, military, and medical facilities. Given the often tight budgets of such institutions, price is certainly a factor, but the potential of clean, quiet, dependable, and effectively inexhaustable electricity regardless of the availability of utility power or oil is a powerful incentive on its own. Many fire stations, police stations, military facilities, and almost all hospitals now have on-site diesel generators capable of automatically supplying electricity should the utility source be out of commission. Obviously, this back-up potential is critical, particularly when emergency functions are threatened by the loss of electricity. The photovoltaic industry has just begun to enter this market with a handful of demonstration projects installed at various government facilities throughout the United States.

Utility companies building centralized photovoltaic facilities to pump power into existing electrical grids will doubtless be one of the largest markets in the continental United States within the next ten years. The three such utility-scale plants in California built in 1982 and 1983 have already pioneered the basics—construction techniques, power-conditioning systems, and the reliability of components are all proven. With existing state and federal tax credits, these projects are clearly competitive with other sources of electricity. But even without such credits, photovoltaic facilities will soon be competitive with conventional sources in much of the United States.

Since utility electricity prices vary widely in this country—for example, two cents per kilowatt hour in parts of the Northwest versus seventeen cents in Manhattan—it is practically impossible to make any clearcut forecast of when and where photovoltaic systems will become competitive. Further complicating the issue are the utilities that have nuclear facilities about to come on-line. In many states these utilities cannot charge customers for the nuclear plant's cost until the plant is generating electricity. When the

United Energy's photovoltaic modules on the firm's own office building rooftop near San Francisco. The water is used to heat the building to varying degrees depending on the weather.

(Source: United Energy Corporation)

charges are passed on to ratepayers, their kilowatt-hour cost may suddenly rise 40 to 90 percent. Such a sudden jump in costs will no doubt result in more conservation and possibly the migration of businesses that require substantial quantities of electricity to other areas with lower costs. Ironically, this cost jump is likely to fuel the market for home photovoltaic systems as well.

During the last ten years, the utility industry has been so revolutionary, and so chaotic, that it appears more willing than ever to try anything that could be termed a positive improvement. What were once the epitome of "blue-chip" corporations with triple-A bond ratings are now widely regarded in the investment community as a mixed bag: some utilities are well managed and have excellent financial records; some, though basically healthy, are riding the thin line between profit and loss; and some are managing their way out of sheer disaster. Although nuclear plants are the source of the industry's most serious financial problems—the approximately forty nuclear plants still under construction will add more than $120 billion to the country's electrical rate base if they are all completed in the early 1990s—cost overruns on coal and hydroelectric

Concentrating and tracking units developed by Martin Marietta and now partially electrifying the Palm Springs City Hall. The entire winglike assemblage turns on its single pier and changes its tilt to follow the sun.

(Source: Southern California Edison)

projects have also caused serious financial problems. And inevitably the financial problems have also triggered a series of legal problems, with state governments, shareholders, local residents, and citizens' groups.

The utility industry's problems can be traced to one source—the clash between its forecasts of future electrical consumption and the realities of the energy crisis of 1973–74. Prior to that pivotal event, the industry had assumed that growth in electrical consumption would continue at a higher rate than population and economic growth, and it used this assumption to justify the construction of more large generating plants. But suddenly that growth curve simply made no sense. Consumption dropped, prices rose, and the growth rate was either less than the national growth rate, about equal, or rising slightly. Forecasts, along with elaborate and very expensive plans for all sorts of new power plants, were rendered so much garbage. The best laid plans were moot in the face of erratic and almost totally unpredictable demand.

The utility industry's troubles have triggered the development of a wide range of new technologies, with entrepreneurs rushing in to fill the need. Since the demand for electricity is both erratic and growing at a slow rate, if at all, the emphasis is now on small-scale power plants of every imaginable type. Thus, a total of 14,193 megawatts of small-scale electrical-generation facilities have been installed or are planned in the United States within only *five* years of this writing. Achieving the same installed capacity within the same time frame—four to seven years—using conventional coal or nuclear plants would be practically impossible.

The trend toward the development of smaller scale utility generating facilities is a response not only to the need for modest incremental expansions of capacity relative to low rates of growth in consumption, but to the peculiar financial constraints of utility companies generally. Most utilities could be characterized as staid, dependable institutions offering a nice modest return to investors who were not interested in risks. Given their reputation as conservative organizations, they were not likely to invest directly in new technologies. A third-party mechanism was needed, a social and financial strategy that would allow the new technology to be built quickly while providing a high return for investors who would not otherwise consider utility investments.

In 1978 Congress passed the Public Utility Regulatory Policies

Act, commonly referred to as PURPA. This act effectively requires utilities to purchase power from small independent power companies. This legislation broke the legal and conceptual monopoly utilities had on electric-power generation, and opened the door for more than 200 new companies to enter the industry. This one piece of legislation, often coupled with solar tax credits, triggered a rapid expansion of generating capacity at lower cost with far less adverse environmental impact, assisted in the development of a number of new industries, and created a substantial number of jobs. PURPA was a breath of fresh air in a stale industry.

How the utility industry will develop photovoltaic facilities is the industry's major unknown. About the only certainty is geographical: owing to both growth and favorable sunshine, the Sunbelt region of the country will probably see the most activity in the development of large-scale photovoltaic plants. Conversely, owing to lower or negative growth, parts of the Northeast, upper Midwest, and New England will remain less suitable for photovoltaic installations on a utility scale in the near-term. Nor will the northwest Pacific coastal area be a suitable area for utility-scale photo-

The first all-solar home in the United States, excluding the thousands of unconventional backwoods homes. This residence is located in Carlisle, Massachusetts. The Solarex polycrystalline panels cover the south-facing roof, generating 7.5 kilowatts, an ample output that would cover every imaginable electrical appliance. The surplus is sold to the utility.

(Source: Steven J. Strong, Solar Design Associates)

voltaic power, both because the region has a long overcast rainy season and because low-cost hydroelectric power dominates there. Sunbelt cities, and many cities in the central Atlantic coast region, are not only sufficiently sunny, they often have air-pollution problems. Although the pollution is due primarily to cars, power plants do contribute to the pall of haze, and every kilowatt produced by a photovoltaic plant represents a net reduction in pollutants.

Adding to the complexity of assessing the potential of photovoltaics for utility-scale plants are a host of issues that have yet to be resolved. The largest is the relationship between utilities and on-site rooftop-mounted photovoltaics. The industry itself appears to be somewhat divided in this area, with some people assuming that the home market will grow slowly because of resistance to change while utilities become primary users of photovoltaics. Others believe that the home market will take off and grow very rapidly simply because of price, but of course that scenario assumes that photovoltaic systems will become so inexpensive they will undercut utility rates by at least 10 to 25 percent in many areas of the country. By the mid-nineties, two other factors will begin to influence the dynamic of utility versus home-photovoltaic systems. In some areas of the country some power plants will be reaching retirement age at about the same time that additional capacity is needed. Thus, utilities will be forced to build new conventional, photovoltaic, or renewable generating facilities. At the same time blackouts or brownouts may increase in frequency

In some cities the mixture of tall and short buildings is such that the large structure casts a shadow over the smaller buildings during a major portion of a typical day (dotted line represents limit of shadow). In this example the entire block is powered by two arrays of PV concentrating units placed in the backyards. Typically, in such a conversion all the neighbors might develop what amounts to their own power company. In the winter the cogenerating units would generate electricity and hot water for bathing and building heat. In the summer much of the hot water would be used to heat a swimming pool. Such a project could be tied into the development of a commons instead of many little-used and confining urban backyards.

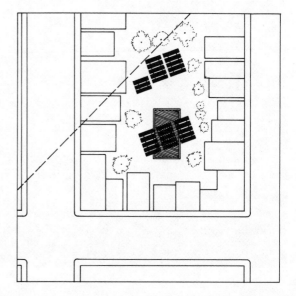

owing to aging equipment, and that could encourage more and more homeowners to buy their own photovoltaic systems. In relation to this entire question of utility versus home-mounted systems, it is conceivable, although fraught with substantial political questions, that the utility companies could become deregulated and thus capable of acting as distributors of electricity—that is, electric-power brokers relative to independent power producers and distributors of home-mounted photovoltaic systems.

Regardless of what happens with utility-scale systems and the market relationships between utility electricity and photovoltaics, it is inevitable that millions of homes will become electrified with photovoltaics. In addition to the 5,000 to 10,000 backwoods cabins already electrified by photovoltaics, more than twenty all-solar homes have been built in the past five years. Many of these houses were designed as demonstration projects, integrating passive and active solar-heating systems with full PV electrical systems. Generally, they tend to be somewhat lavish in their electrical consumption in order to demonstrate that one need not sacrifice any convenience with solar electricity. Since these homes were not intended to be market-priced units, and photovoltaics were then too expensive anyway, no attempt was made to size the photovoltaic system relative to the home's possible price. Nevertheless, regardless of prices that exceeded $200,000, two of these demonstration houses sold within twenty-four hours of going on the market.

In the late seventies and early eighties a number of wealthy

In many suburban and rural locations, homes or commercial structures located on a north-facing slope may not have sufficient sunlight for solar heat or electricity. A concentrating or simple PV array could be located in the nearest open area and jointly owned by a cluster of houses. It could supply just electricity or hot water and electricity.

In countless instances a home is sheltered by huge trees that a homeowner or neighborhood may not want to remove or trim. Indeed, in some areas of the country trees are a primary means of cooling in the hot summers. A PV array can be located in the backyard, well away from the trees and in full, clear sun.

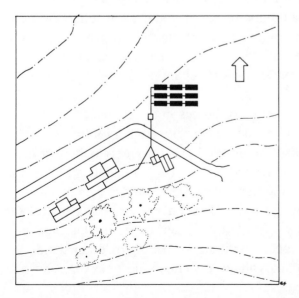

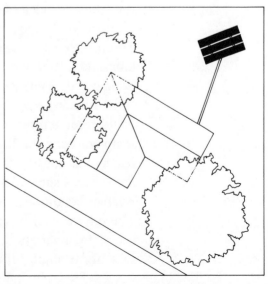

people began building homes in relatively remote areas. Their reasons varied, but most of these people expressed a common view that the world's economy was shaky and their own way of life too reliant upon economic trends over which they had no control. In response to this tentative if not downright bleak vision, many of these people built homes that were all but totally self-contained. The designs incorporated spring- or well-fed water systems, small-scale hydro- or wind-powered electric systems, and a variety of solar- and wood-energy schemes to keep the houses warm no matter what. Most of these people did not want anyone to know where their houses were.

At present, an entertainer is building a home in the mountains of Nevada that will include 10,000 square feet of interior space, large exterior decks, an Olympic-size swimming pool, tennis courts, a small barn, and parking for his five cars. The entire complex will be 100 percent solar, powered by a large photovoltaic system. He's even considering an electric car that would be recharged by photovoltaics so he will not have to buy gas for his regular trips to the local casino and airport. The cost of this retreat has not been revealed, but it is likely to be in the $1 million range.

Obviously, most of us are not going to be building such lavish homes, but it is increasingly likely that a growing number of wealthy homeowners will incorporate photovoltaics into new homes or modify their existing homes to accept photovoltaic power systems. Furthermore, we may see the development of relatively small and exclusive real estate projects that incorporate photovoltaics. The very idea of a totally, or almost totally, self-reliant home is appealing to those among us who are highly security conscious. Those who have made millions of dollars, or even hundreds of thousands, tend to be extremely self-reliant people who take pride in their independence.

Estimates as to the number of homes in the United States that could receive most or all of their electricity from a rooftop PV system vary between 20 and 30 million homes, roughly a third of the residential housing in the United States. The remaining structures are in areas such as Seattle that receive less sun due to regional weather conditions, are located in deep pockets or on north slopes where they receive only a few hours of sun, or are limited in solar access by a variety of local conditions—shading by other buildings, for example. If photovoltaics eventually become very cheap,

A new south-facing structure built to maximize solar gain with PV electricity integrated into the building's design. It contains a large greenhouse space that captures heat and serves as a planting area. Interior plants can act as biological air-refreshing systems. The building's side walls are partially covered with earth to minimize heat loss. North-facing skylights with PV panels atop their south faces allow indirect daylight to flood the structure. Before the days of saturation fluorescent lighting, most factory structures had sawtooth roofs with skylights. Some daylight is *always* better than all-electric light.

and amorphous cells present that possibility, then it is conceivable that even houses receiving little sun would be capable of generating a portion of their electricity from PVs. As noted earlier, there are also numerous possibilities for block- or neighborhood-scaled photovoltaic systems that might be located to maximize solar access while feeding power to houses in shady areas.

Any photovoltaic system, regardless of its size, requires various electrical components to modulate and, in some cases, store electricity. There are three technical strategies involved in electrifying a home with photovoltaics: stand-alone systems with batteries are the most expensive, utility-backed systems with some storage capacity are in the middle range, and utility-interactive systems with no storage and the ability to pump power back into the utility grid are the least expensive. Of the total cost, the actual photovoltaic modules may account for anywhere from 40 to 60 percent of the system cost, with inverters, power-conditioning equipment, and batteries accounting for the remainder. The average cost, in 1985, of the three systems is about $18 per peak watt. Typically, this yields a total system cost (including installation) for an average suburban house in the $30,000 to $60,000 range, assuming no alterations in consumption patterns.

Large utility-scaled systems in the 1-megawatt or greater range allow lower costs due to the ratio between cost of photovoltaics and comparatively inexpensive power-conditioning equipment. Clearly, this economy of scale will be a market force affecting the homeowner's choice of buying a system. At this time, no clear trend is emerging that might favor one approach over the other. Although cost reductions in photovoltaics due to improved efficiency and mass production will lower costs for both utilities and homeowners, there is no way to know if similar cost reductions might be possible with more efficient and mass-produced power-conditioning and storage technology.

Developments in power-conditioning and battery-storage technology have tended to lag behind that of photovoltaics. As a result, we have yet to see whole systems of maximum efficiency composed of components produced on a mass-production line. It is quite conceivable that higher levels of production would result in dramatic reductions in a system's non-PV costs, and these reductions may not be applicable to utility-scale plants, since they would tend to relate to custom-built facilities not constructed on a mass-market scale.

The already tangled complex of market forces that will influence the development of home-mounted photovoltaic cells is even further complicated by two other potential markets—those of industry and transportation. These markets could become highly active due to, of all things, air pollution.

Historically, there are many precedents for environmental pollution forcing a technological shift, most recently the rush of interest in electric cars that surfaced in the late sixties and early seventies. The energy crisis forced us to build smaller and more efficient cars, inherently less polluting, although in spite of the change air pollution has generally worsened. Traffic conditions in many U.S. cities will soon be much more congested as freeways reach their capacity, and pollution will get worse—fast. It will then become clear that a widely used nonpolluting vehicle is necessary. With the dual need to remain competitive by building low-cost transportation and to produce truly nonpolluting cars, the automotive industry could be forced to develop cheap electric "citycars" designed to be recharged from photovoltaic panels mounted on a house or garage. If such cars were widely used in cities, we could radically reduce air pollution, eventually eliminating it entirely.

Air pollution might also be a deciding factor in the industrial market's judgment to purchase photovoltaics. PVs have already become common on the industrial fringes—in charging caboose batteries, pumping water, and powering communications systems—and as the price goes down the technology will no doubt be used on factories and commercial structures as well. As described earlier, PVs at remote sites are most valued for their reliability and simplicity, but as the technology moves into mainstream use prices will have to come down substantially. Industrial and commercial markets will tend toward more sophisticated photovoltaic systems, often incorporated into a building's architecture. Cogenerating photovoltaic modules with concentrating cells and hot-water generation may become a mainstay of commercial installations. Diesel cogenerating facilities now being installed could be replaced by photovoltaic cogeneration systems in 8 to 15 years—significantly reducing pollution.

Backwoods and Global Markets

Don was a hippie who moved to the coastal mountains in the late sixties. By 1980 the odd jobs he'd survived on were fewer and further between, and besides, his truck had shocks like sticks in tubes. The roads were rough and his life was rougher. His land was so steep no one would buy it. His truck was barely worth scrap price. Don was slipping back into entropy, or at least that's what it felt like.

Don had grown a few plants for his own use so it was not difficult to increase the crop by a few hundred percent. He did and did it well. One year later he walked into the hardware store and peeled off a few 100 dollar bills for a new drip-irrigation system. He rolled bills like he'd once rolled tobacco. He bought things—new shocks, a ton of books, and a new water pump.

In the middle of the small town Don frequented was a tiny store sandwiched between two fast-food stands. The place was so small you could read *Mother Earth News* on the stand while picking out the tools to make it real with your left hand. The place was called the "Real Tool Company," and it sold all manner of gardening tools, homesteading tools, and alternative-energy reading tools—that is, guidebooks to the New Age.

Don had been using kerosene lights and a 12-volt car battery to power his stereo tape deck, but no matter how he looked at it the system just didn't make it. Electricity from the nearest power line was simply out of the question. Besides, if the power company strung a wire out to Don's house they'd see a lot more than trees: too many crops were hidden in the forest. Photovoltaics were clearly the answer.

The ARCO Solar sales representative knew exactly what a market niche looks like, acts like, and feels like. He spent an afternoon watching a few local growers come into the Real Tool Company, and he knew he had hit a market niche. The deal was struck in a few hours and Real Tools now handled a new line of photovoltaics.

Next fall arrived, the harvest was good, and most of the growers came in to buy their PVs before winter set in. Don bought four modules, six small 12-volt bulbs, fixtures, wiring, batteries, and a power-control panel. He'd moved to the country to escape the ravages of overtechnologized cities and now here he was reading under lights powered by crystal cells transforming sunlight and made by an oil company. What a long strange trip it's been.

Photovoltaics have changed the lives of many backwoods residents in the United States—as noted earlier, a U.S. phenomenon that contains within it global implications. Electricity is not evenly spread throughout the world. It is consistently developed in industrialized countries and inconsistently developed everywhere else.

A remote mountain residence in the coastal mountains of Southern California, near Santa Barbara. The home's sole source of electricity is the sun, via ARCO Solar modules standing apart from the house. This photograph dramatically illustrates just how little technology is needed to provide electricity.

(Source: ARCO Solar)

The United States, Canada, and Europe, as well as parts of Japan and Asia, have the most developed and sophisticated electrification systems. Composed of mature technologies, these systems would cost hundreds of billions if built today. Although the cities of the world, with very few exceptions, have large-scale generating systems, the spread of these systems varies widely, with many barely extending beyond the suburbs. Countless villages utilize all sorts of small-scale power plants, for continuous or intermittent electricity. Diesel electric generator sets dominate this market. In many rural areas there is either no power at all, an occasionally used generator system, a modest supply from a nearby industrial plant, or the trickle of power from one wire at the end of the utility grid.

In the 1930s a young movie star named Henry Fonda played a worker on a high-tension-wire team installing long-distance high-voltage cables strung from tall steel towers. The men on the "highline" were shown wearing outsized insulating gloves, using 3-foot wrenches as deftly as if they were .45 Colts, all while manhandling 5-foot-tall insulators 200 feet over the desert. The imagery was of man conquering the wilderness, bringing the magic of electricity to

A modest backwoods cabin outfitted with a small photovoltaic panel. An installation on this scale requires only a few batteries and a simple 12-volt DC electric system. Most of the necessary components are available at marine or RV-supply stores and the entire system could be installed for less than $700.

(Source: Mobil Solar Energy Corporation)

the dark wilderness world of farmers and small towns. It characterized the rural-electrification program under the Roosevelt administration in the 1930s.

During the forties, fifties, and sixties, the United States
advanced this progressive vision of electrification through various
foreign aid programs, and the vision remains a driving force
behind contemporary aid programs today. Typically, the plan
involves a developing nation building some vast new centralized
generating facility, often a large hydroelectric dam, with loans
from the industrialized countries through such agencies as the
United Nations and World Bank. Predictably, the developing nation
then buys the plant's components from the lender country, or countries, and continues to buy all the industrial and consumer technology it can then, in theory, afford because of the economic uplift
stimulated by the initial investment. Electrification, often in combination with irrigation, is viewed as the key that will open the doors
to a new economy.

International aid in the form of capital-intensive, long-term
investments in such sophisticated technology as electrical generation is fraught with hidden social, political, economic, and environmental consequences. A seemingly simple effort by the United
States to build a hydroelectric dam in a tropical jungle may be
"sold" in the local press as a benevolent gesture of goodwill, when
in fact it is really a response to a nearby Soviet facility. The press
release for a coal-burning power plant to be built with World Bank
funds in a remote corner of an Asian island makes no mention of a
huge multinational corporation's plans to develop a zinc mine 4
miles away. And the local agenda behind a project's development
may involve a few up-and-coming politicians in need of a sizeable,
working, and expensive power plant to impress the masses. Certainly there are benevolent gestures, but as often as not the motiva-
tion is economic or political, quite understandable given the implications of electricity as a social and economic force.

In the 1940s and early 1950s, a small country in Africa or Asia
had relatively few choices when it went shopping for engineering
assistance and financing for a new power plant. The United States,
Canada, and a few European countries were effectively the only
sources of talent, technology, and money all in one place. In terms
of foreign policy, political philosophy, technological choices, and
corporate involvement, the deal was simple—you bought the sell-

er's package. Since the 1960s, however, the deals have become much more complex, as countries such as Japan, Korea, Brazil, India, South Africa, and the Soviet Union have become participants in the aid- and technology-transfer game. This transition, from a seller's to a buyer's market, signifies a move away from the dominance of European and American technologies and the strategic approach to development that often went with those technologies.

International aid for the development of electrification often presupposed that most countries of the world would want to emulate the United States. Until recently many did, but there is a growing recognition among many planners within Third World nations that they cannot afford to emulate the U.S. model of electrification. The sheer cost of building U.S.- or European-style electrification systems is a major barrier when the regional, national, and world economies are all changing simultaneously in almost totally unpredictable ways. In El Salvador, President Duarte speaks of citizens who will not stop for stop signs for fear of being robbed or murdered by streetcorner criminals. Obviously, in such a social context it is questionable whether one is even living in a civilization, let alone a culture capable of building a complex electrification scheme. While the situation in El Salvador is certainly extreme, it illustrates a condition common throughout much of the world—chaos. Yet the need remains, and the value of electrification as a means of spreading solutions to political and economic problems is very high. Electricity allows communication and a degree of economic well-being that appear to be universally

Comparison of a distribution system in an industrialized country with that in a less developed country. In industrialized countries, electricity tends to be evenly distributed and generally more equitably priced, covering all major population centers linked by highways (line). Moreover, the population density is low. Less developed areas commonly have small grid systems concentrated only in some urban zones. Many villages (black dots) have little or no electricity, and parts of the big cities may also have little or none. The proportional relationship among cities and the centers of outlying areas tends to be more disparate; there are very large cities covering vast areas and very small villages scattered over the countryside. Conventional generating systems installed in this context almost always result in the location of more population and industry in cities that are already too large for their own infrastructures to support. Decentralized PV electricity is thus a very strong potential for village-electrification schemes that do not exacerbate the existing urban population problems.

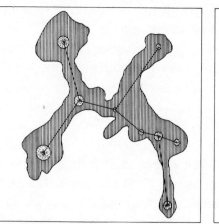
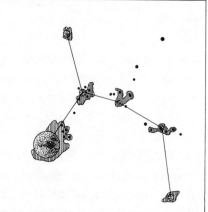

regarded improvements in the quality of life.

Cities are like factories of vital commercial activity providing products and services of every imaginable form. Cities are the centers of economic and cultural wealth, and as a species we are nearly obsessed with building them. Throughout the world, the flight from rural regions to cities is threatening to break the economic back of countless regions. The cities are where the cultural activity, the possibilities for a better future, exist. And most cities are dependably electrified.

Rural electrification is thus more than just a means of elevating the cultural and economic life of country and often poor people. It is a key element in a strategy aimed at stemming the tide of people filling already overcrowded cities.

At the very least, electrification will allow a degree of communication—television and telephones—that would not exist otherwise. At best it can foster all sorts of small-scale agricultural and industrial enterprises that would not need to rely upon centralized—which means urban in the minds of most people—electric power sources. Photovoltaics are perfectly suited to the task of providing decentralized electricity in thousands of small villages.

John F. Kennedy's Peace Corps of the 1960s helped to accelerate a movement toward what came to be called appropriate technology, or AT. AT covers everything from village water pumps of the most elegant and simple design, to solar stills, to remote satellite receiver stations allowing a small village to pick up educational television programs. The emphasis of AT is using a little of what is at hand, a lot of local knowledge, a pinch of imported technology, and maybe a prayer from the local shaman. In contrast to huge megabuck electrification projects, appropriate technology emphasizes an approach that begins where people are—technically, economically, and culturally. It is inherently entrepreneurial in that it teaches a way to bootstrap an economy as an independent entity, not as a dependent upon international welfare or corporate largesse. Unfortunately, AT is all too often ignored by politicians, who are frequently more interested in Cadillacs than bicycles.

Since the mid-sixties, we have seen a vacillation in the world of foreign aid and electrification among large centralized projects, the latest model diesel generator, and anything that will work for a few months. In much of the Third World, this vacillation has hardened into a deadlock: financial and political instability, if not debts to the World Bank, practically eliminates the possibility of large-scale electrification, while at the same time politicians are much less interested than before in developing village-scale electrical-generating facilities of no monumental value in gaining political office. So nothing happens.

In many countries electrification is a symbol of the first step towards a dramatic improvement in the quality of life. But if this step requires the commitment of billions in foreign aid, endless dependence upon foreign creditors, and social uncertainties that could threaten the government's existence, then the cost may be too high. In this way, electrification can become an enormous barrier, a wall between a life of poverty and at least the possibility of some improvement.

There is a new element in the game, one that has crept up slowly from behind. It is the world's familiarity with electronics. This new element has set the stage for photovoltaic development.

Americans of the 1920s knew what electrical-power stations looked like because there was one in the neighborhood. American industrialization is a history of dominant technologies—cars, planes, telephones, computers—that have infected the nation's consciousness with a lexicon of terminology and a literature of affectionate relationship to tools. Nowhere on Earth has there been such a preoccupation with machines of every imaginable form. Our language is filled with words and concepts—dune buggy, skimobile, data link, gigawatt, control rod, modem, mouse—that are entirely the result of technological developments.

A child in the United States learns technology through the concepts of the dominant tool of the time. In 1880, the brass-trimmed locomotive steaming into town at the head end of the express spoke of progress and worlds beyond the confines of back fences and corner candy stores. In 1980, the computer in an eleven-year-old's bedroom glows at 10 P.M. as the child travels into yet another realm far beyond the confines of Saturday morning cartoons. The technology is, as always, just a dead object. But tools almost always embody not only the cultural information of the maker but the visions and dreams of the user. They are mirrors of our existence, metaphors for our hopes, and the currency of cultural exchange.

A child in Indonesia in 1980 might see a train only occasionally. Cars are a common sight but financially inaccessible to much of the population. But electronics are everywhere, very accessible and very direct as currency of cultural exchange. Children of the world know portable radios, tape players, and televisions like children of the United States in 1965 knew '55 Chevvies. Names like Sony, Toshiba, Panasonic, Sanyo, and Fuji cut across cultural and language barriers just as Ford, General Motors, General Electric, and Westinghouse once did.

Practically everyone on the planet knows what a television is, a remarkable fact considering that the TV was invented only half a century ago on a back street in San Francisco. And in the most remote outpost, the seemingly innocent portable radio is not only a channel into the world of radio signals coming from God knows where but also a tool that requires an occasional infusion of small cylinders of electric fuel. The radio or television's design, how it feels, and the look of its internal circuitry all represent a language of electronics. And the channel one tunes into not only provides a broad range of information and entertainment, it provides at least a sense of how others live in places far away. While many countries maintain excessive control over the airwaves, censoring much of what is available on the world media market, the widespread popularity of rock-and-roll is a testament to the power of electronic tools and to the near impossibility of censorship when there's so much "in the air."

In short, electronics is the world's most widespread technological language. The point of access for much of the world's population is the local general store, the equivalent of that truly amazing American phenomenon, the hardware store. Indoor plumbing may be an odd idea, electricity may be fluctuating according to the whims of whomever is in political power that month, and gas lines may be so long the last car in line will cost more to fill up because of inflation during the time it was in line. But regardless of these daily problems, and almost regardless of geographical location, the local hardware cum variety store will be doing a steady business in electronic parts, tape decks, radios, televisions, calculators, watches, and shoebox-sized electric pianos. Rock-and-roll over a Sony is as ubiquitous as Coca-Cola signs.

The introduction of any new technology strikes the resonant and dynamic chords of fear and desire in most of us. The least sensitive buy the latest issue and use it with no reservations whatsoever. The most sensitive buy it, think about it awhile, use it with reserve, but use it anyway. To the extent that the new tool arrives in a familiar box, with familiar markings and parts, it is received as a tool of value that is not strange and out of place.

Projects on the scale of Egypt's Aswan Dam not only require vast sums of money and decades to build, but they come in very unusual packages that require training and education efforts nearly as big as the dam itself. Indeed, as is often the case with highly sophisticated technology requiring legions of specialized technicians to build and operate, huge electrification projects can add immeasurably to the tendency to centralize political power among a sophisticated elite. The tool responds to a tendency towards elite oligarchy and it feeds it at the same time. Typically, this contributes to the economic and cultural dislocations the project is often intended to solve. And in many cases it results in a powerful linkage between the ruling technocrats of a small country and their counterparts within a large developed country. Inevitably such a link splits their allegiance, with one portion going to their own people in their own neighborhoods, and another to their mentors in some far off city.

In contrast to these huge projects with their endless repercussions, the photovoltaic cell is a simple and accessible device that utilizes relatively familiar components. Although more sophisticated than many appropriate-technology projects, photovoltaics are nonetheless highly appropriate in scale and installation to undeveloped nations. They do not inherently require massive social changes or physical dislocations. Nor do they require that an endless dependency be developed with some alien culture. PVs can be purchased now and installed immediately. PVs are a consumer product, not a political process, so buying electricity does not become an exercise in capitalist, Marxist, socialist, monarchist, or communist politics. Rather, it remains in the realm of plain old ordinary free enterprise—the force that keeps us all alive while the governments of the world fiddle with economic theories.

Japan imports more than 90 percent of its energy in the form of natural gas, oil, coal, and uranium. It also produces some of the best in automobiles, electronic devices, industrial machinery, railroad equipment, ships, tractors, toys, and office machines. Japan is like a ship at sea—it depends on outside sources of fuel to continue its journey. In a world where energy sources are becoming steadily less secure, Japan has no choice but to ensure its survival by remaining extraordinarily competitive in world markets, while simultaneously developing any and all possible indigenous energy sources. The value it adds to every one of its boggling array of products is not just a measure of its people's industriousness but also proof of the critical importance of high quality to maintaining leadership and surviving in world markets. Unlike the United States, Japan has no major local source of energy, nothing to fall back on if oil or coal shipments are disrupted.

Although the Japanese nuclear-power industry has not been plagued with the problems of its U.S. counterpart, the sheer cost and time involved in building nuclear plants effectively preclude their further development in Japan on any substantial scale. Solar energy is somewhat developed there, particularly in the form of hot-water and space heating in southern Japan, but it has yet to become a major source of energy. In the larger cities, Japan's dependency on oil and coal-fired electrical generation is ruining the purity of the country's air, while continuing a risky dependency on Middle East oil and U.S. coal.

As a people, a government, and a series of corporate entities,

A small desalinization plant near Jeddah, Saudi Arabia. The country has an enormous quantity of oil, and sunshine that never stops. Saudi Arabia has made a number of major investments in photovoltaic plants, whole power systems, and PV research.

(Source: Mobil Solar Energy Corporation)

the Japanese are formidable competition. While our government works with corporate management in a state of dynamic tension, the Japanese government works with corporate managers through a formal series of allegiances. We might be able to delude ourselves into thinking that the "energy crisis" is over and that we can sit back and discuss energy issues while the shovels devour Wyoming's coal—and its landscape. But the Japanese do not remember a time when energy was not a central issue, often the driving force of their nation's foreign policy. If there is one issue about which there is little argument in Japan, it is that Japan *must* maintain its lead as a powerful manufacturer and trading nation. There is only time enough to debate *how* to do it, not whether to do it, and energy is the critical ingredient.

By comparison, the United States is like an entrepreneur. The paradox of entrepreneurship: to secure financial backing, entrepreneurs must reveal the proprietary information on which their potential wealth rests. Yet in doing so the entrepreneur risks losing the knowledge to a competitor. Nothing ventured, nothing gained. As a nation, we have invented wave upon wave of technological and cultural innovations. The time lapse between our export of those innovations and the importing people's full utilization and then manufacture of the innovation has grown smaller and smaller with each successive wave. With photovoltaics, we barely started the industry before Japanese and European companies jumped in with both feet.

Japan's photovoltaic industry is now a formidable contender in the world market. Until recently, U.S. photovoltaic companies had not even manufactured amorphous cells, but the Japanese have already built a substantial industry in amorphous cells for consumer products. Hondas, Subarus, and Toyotas will probably all contain amorphous battery-charging panels before U.S. manufacturers begin installing these panels in cars.

The competition between the United States and Japan in consumer electronics, communications, and computers has been a major impetus to innovation on both sides of the Pacific. Simultaneously, it has been a quiet forum for the sharing of knowledge, at least until that knowledge becomes saleable. At that point, research teams become companies, proprietary protection increases, and the race is on. The stakes of the game are so high that even the temptation to steal is overwhelming, and stories of midnight raids, corporate spies, and deals at research conferences are not uncommon. We say: "If we don't do it the Japanese will, and they'll get the market." Undoubtedly, the Japanese say the same thing, only more quietly.

As Detroit auto makers know all too well, the Japanese are keenly perceptive when it comes to new markets. It is a perception of opportunity as clear and clean as the layered steel edge of an ancient samuri sword.

There is no doubt the Japanese perceive the world market for photovoltaics—it's too big to miss. It is likely that their leap from first-generation crystal to third-generation amorphous-cell technology within only a few years was motivated by the perfect alignment between the power needs of small calculators, regions where many of those devices are sold, and the enormous market for electrification in those regions. The same person in Sri Lanka who bought a Sanyo battery-powered radio in 1975 might buy a Sanyo solar-powered radio in 1985. In 1990, being familiar with solar energy as a concept, the same person might buy Sanyo amorphous photovoltaic panels. And the same process might begin in countless areas where even battery-powered electronics are difficult to maintain. In such cases, the first electronic device might be a solar-powered one. This sequence of relationships is all the more potent given the already extensive retail markets through which all manner of Japanese electronics are sold worldwide.

From the Japanese standpoint, the photovoltaic technology has nearly miraculous implications. First, the Japanese have the means and experience to excel in the production of photovoltaics. Next, by using photovoltaics in their existing consumer electronic products they can add to the marketability of those products—gaining markets in areas where batteries—not to mention power lines—might be inaccessible. And the sale of photovoltaic products worldwide not only sets the stage for the sale of photovoltaic home-power systems, it could open the door to applications in all manner of other electrified technology, right on up to automobiles and trains.

Meanwhile, within Japan photovoltaics at the very least present the possibility of eliminating the country's dependency on outside energy sources. By combining photovoltaics with other renewable technologies, over a period of two to three decades, Japan could become reliant upon sustainable energy sources. That possibility alone would be sufficient to accelerate Japan's development of its photovoltaic technology.

European and U.S. corporations engaged in photovoltaic development and marketing perceive this relationship between consumer products and electrification and are responding to it, but their need is not so pressing as Japan's, nor are their international reputations in electronics so great. Unlike the Japanese, Americans and Europeans tend to see energy as a peripheral issue, not the organizing, elemental economic force that it is. While people within the photovoltaic industry in the United States might perceive the staggering economic and social import of photovoltaic technology on the global scale, many U.S. politicians remain bound by the notion that energy is an issue to be discussed by technicians. To the Japanese, and to much of the Asian world, it is not merely energy that is at issue, but dependency. To Americans, and to a lesser extent to Europeans, the questions remain abstract: Domestic or imported? Which corporation? What fuel? and to what degree are we going to be dependent?

It is already widely assumed in the U.S. photovoltaic industry that if the federal government does not continue supporting photovoltaic development by as many means as possible we will lose our current market leadership, probably to the Japanese. While we will no doubt remain major players, it will be most difficult to regain, and maintain, the lead without a measure of government support approximately equal to that given the Japanese and European industries.

This situation with respect to photovoltaic technology and its development worldwide brings into focus one of the most critical issues for the future of the United States. Are we declining as an innovator *and* a producer of new technology, or are we coming to occupy a cultural niche on the world scene as Earth's major entrepreneur? Is our country becoming the cultural workshop and technological laboratory in which all manner of innovation is created— only to be produced elsewhere? Hopefully we are only going through a major cultural and economic transition that will result in increasingly competitive U.S. industries.

China: One Gargantuan Marketplace

The liberalizing reforms underway in China in recent years have unleashed an entrepreneurial spirit long dormant, and a thousand markets have bloomed across China. The explosion of free enterprise has had profound implications, both positive and negative, for the Chinese, but its effects in China may pale by comparison to those upon the world at large. Most people know all too well what happens when a new country joins the industrialized world's trading club. And we all know the ramifications of using a large pool of cheap labor to produce very good products. The impact of China upon the world is not only inevitable, it is inevitably enormous.

China's re-emergence into world trade coincides with a period in history when a diverse array of competing electrical-generating technologies exist side by side. China is incompletely electrified, and many of its central generating stations are old coal burners with little or no pollution-control equipment. If China is to become more industrialized, and more competitive on world markets, it will have to develop new sources of electricity while minimizing the negative impacts of this expansion. Since the mid-seventies, three possibilities have emerged. First, with assistance from foreign firms, planning and development work on new coal power plants has begun. Next, in late 1984 and early 1985, China reached agreement with Hong Kong interests to construct a nuclear plant, probably to be built with French technology. And, third, in 1984 U.S. photovoltaic firms began serious talks with Chinese officials interested in PV factories. If photovoltaic production goes forward, as appears likely, PV production will probably be well established before the proposed nuclear plant is completed in 1992–93.

The population distribution of China is "finer grained" than that of much of the world. While Chinese cities are large and dense, the countryside is evenly developed with thousands of small villages. The country is unusually reliant upon rural farm life, and always vulnerable to the inevitable drawing power of cities, with their increasingly free and culturally diverse markets. In such a context the development of centralized electricity would tend to be focused on cities, and not rural villages, which would require a vast and very expensive grid system to reach. As a result, expanded electrification would only add to the attractions of cities. It would seem, then, that China has a powerful incentive to develop photovoltaics—with their potential for the quick, inexpensive powering of rural areas—as a primary, if not *the* primary, means of electrification.

At this time it is not clear if the Chinese have a specific strategy for electrification. Actions so far suggest that the Chinese government is pursuing a number of options simultaneously and is waiting to see which technology, or what combination of technologies, offers the broadest range of advantages at the least cost.

If the Chinese do indeed opt for photovoltaics, they are highly likely to become major producers for the foreign as well as domestic market. It could take eight, ten, possibly fifteen years before they are major competitors, but their entry appears inevitable.

China will formally take over Hong Kong in 1997. Hong Kong is nearly legendary as a center for creative entrepreneurs. It is a capitalist greenhouse filled with innovation, wealth, and the brutal honesty of a free market—in everything. The capitalists in Hong Kong do not miss new markets. China appears to be moving towards a policy of treating Hong Kong as its Manhattan on the Pacific Rim.

McDonald's Restaurants, Spire Corporation, and PVs Everywhere

McDonald's doesn't just sell hamburgers, it sells businesses. Anyone, anywhere, with the necessary capital and minimal business credentials can purchase a McDonald's franchise and go into business. McDonald's management does not care whether the menu is in French, Spanish, Italian—or Chinese—so long as the hamburgers are cooked right and sold in the appropriate package. Thus, the sale of billions upon billions of Big Macs represents not merely an astounding business success, but a cultural phenomenon. Regardless of one's personal taste for McDonald's food, it is impossible to deny that this one restaurant chain speaks for an American aspect of life almost everywhere. Obviously, wherever a McDonald's is built there is already a high degree of awareness as to what McDonald's represents. The nearly simultaneous development of many McDonald's in many places is certainly the result of intense advertising and massive sales volume, but it may also be a case of McDonald's being . . . in the air.

Many American corporations remain stuck in the notion that they should only sell a completed product to other nations, not the entire means of production. Rather than believe that there is enough—market, jobs, and technology—for everyone, they choose to believe that they must control, or attempt to control, the dissemination of technology. But in this age of chaotic and interdependent global relationships, a corporation, industry, even a nation that attempts to own a particular technology will end up in the dust. Other countries are no longer interested in and accepting of an endless stream of consumer goods produced elsewhere; they know what that kind of dependency means. Just as there is a growing movement in the United States toward employee stock ownership, there is a growing movement in the world favoring technologies and social strategies that will allow both the spread of the technology and the creation of an industrial base to produce it.

The photovoltaic industry is barely ten years old, if one dates its emergence as an industry at 1975. Yet in that very short time, and despite or because of various debates about the most appropriate means of generating electricity, photovoltaic technology has spread to many points around the planet.

Roger Little is the president and founder of a small photovoltaic company called Spire Corporation. Mr. Little wants Spire to become the McDonald's of photovoltaics.

Roger Little's strategy did not come about by a whim, or by a detailed analysis of what might happen in the world based on academic data. Rather, he built his plan on a brutally honest appraisal of what a small company like Spire could do in a new industry that had the implications of PVs. The resulting strategy not only responds to trends typified by joint ventures and McDonald's extremely rapid development around the planet; it is modeled on a method that could foster the nearly simultaneous development worldwide of the photovoltaic industry—or any industry for that matter.

In the early eighties, Spire had developed both photovoltaic cells and the production machinery to make the cells. It was clear that the global market was enormous, so Spire went to venture

An all-solar home located in the wooded lands of southeastern Massachusetts, using a 4.5-kilowatt PV system with utility interconnection. The home generates a surplus of electricity, which is sold to the local utility. The home is solar heated—space and water—and has a solar greenhouse and earth berms (mounds of earth against the building's wall, visible at left) to reduce heating demands in winter.

(Source: Steven J. Strong, Solar Design Associates)

capitalists to raise money. The response: "How can you and your small company possibly compete with huge oil companies that can afford to sink hundreds of millions into a venture for ten years or more before seeing any return at all?" What could one entrepreneur say?

No answer on Little's part, no matter how well thought out, could possibly reduce the disparity between Spire and ARCO, Mobil, Shell, and Standard of Ohio. And photovoltaic technology in the United States was still too heavily governed by dubious government subsidies that could suddenly change with a whim of Congress and wreck the PV industry. Still, the machines existed to make cells, producing the entire module on a relatively simple production line. Little's idea was to sell the entire factory in a joint-venture arrangement somewhat analogous to a McDonald's franchise. The oil companies would not do that.

Pakistan's government and private industry leaders have little interest in the U.S. balance-of-trade deficit, in whether we have 8 or 20 percent unemployment, or in whether we are building nuclear or eating tofu. Rather, Pakistan's leaders are concerned that the

Not a deep freeze but a module-encapsulating machine. The nearly complete module is placed under the cover and sheets of encapsulating plastic material are placed over it. Closing the top allows sufficient vacuum to be drawn, eliminating air trapped in the module, and the encapsulant material is bonded to the module.

(Source: Spire Corporation)

lack of electricity in much of their country is unquestionably the largest, seemingly most impenetrable barrier to *any* improvement in the quality of life there. If one assumes that a central grid and large centralized power plants are the needed ingredients, the barrier to such improvement amounts to billions of dollars and decades of time. If one assumes that Pakistan can import photovoltaics, the barrier is lowered to hundreds of millions and perhaps two decades. But if one assumes that Pakistan can buy factories and produce its own photovoltaics, at its own labor rates, then the barrier to nearly total electrification is down to tens of millions and maybe fifteen years before much of the country is electrified. From the Pakistani standpoint, what was a deal of multibillion dollar proportions, with inherent problems of environmental risks and long-term dependence on another culture, has suddenly become a deal of far smaller proportions and one that will trigger the development of a whole sequence of other industrial and cultural changes with practically no environmental risks. Pakistan is now proceeding with plans to purchase Spire photovoltaic facilities and other renewable technology.

Spire Corporation has already sold photovoltaic manufacturing equipment to companies throughout the United States and in Japan, Australia, Southeast Asia, India, Saudi Arabia, North Africa, Italy, England, and Brazil. The sale of manufacturing equipment and supplies, or whole factories, is a strategy that is very likely to result in Spire Corporation becoming the McDonald's of the photovoltaic industry.

Spire makes the various machines used to transform raw silicon wafers into a finished module composed of four to forty cells and ready to be installed. Spire's machines are the basic elements of their largest product, a 40-by-80-foot photovoltaic-manufacturing plant capable of producing 1 megawatt of photovoltaic cells annually. In the United States, 1 megawatt might electrify 200 to 400 homes, but in much of the Third World that output might translate into electric power to more than 1000 homes. Spire sells the whole package—its own machines, various ancillary devices, and the technical training to go with it. In exchange Spire receives a portion of the new company's equity and an agreement to supply the new firm with raw wafers from which the cells and modules are made. Beyond the initial arrangement, Spire also intends to assist the firms it has "seeded" in later transitions—to the more sophisti-

The "Tabber," built by Spire Corporation. It automatically solders the small metal tab onto a PV cell, allowing the cell to be wired into a full module.

(Source: Spire Corporation)

A machine for testing finished PV modules. Testing in full sunlight is certainly workable but doing so involves difficulty in judging the precise output relative to atmospheric moisture and varying light conditions. This machine subjects the complete module to intense white light with specific characteristics. The terminal, at right, allows the operator to chart the modules' performance under changing light conditions.

(Source: Spire Corporation)

cated manufacturing process for amorphous cells and to other key steps in developing a photovoltaic industry, notably silicon production.

The three machines that Spire has perfected are the cell tabber, laminator, and tester. Although many of the mechanical and electronic components of these machines are very sophisticated, the finished machines appear ordinary, even innocuous. The tabber automatically solders small metal tabs onto incoming solar cells. The tabs allow each cell to be wired into a module with other cells. The laminator bonds the cells into a solid sheet by the use of sheet encapsulants such as ethylene vinyl acetate. The laminator looks like a large home freezer with a top-opening lid. The tester is a large box that imitates the sun. Internal sensors can detect the module's output relative to a consistent and known quantity of photons—light. The addition of a few more basic machines, some production tables, sufficient water and electricity, and twelve employees, and you're in business. The entire factory, even including building materials, could fit into a few standard international freight containers. With the addition of a photovoltaic and battery-

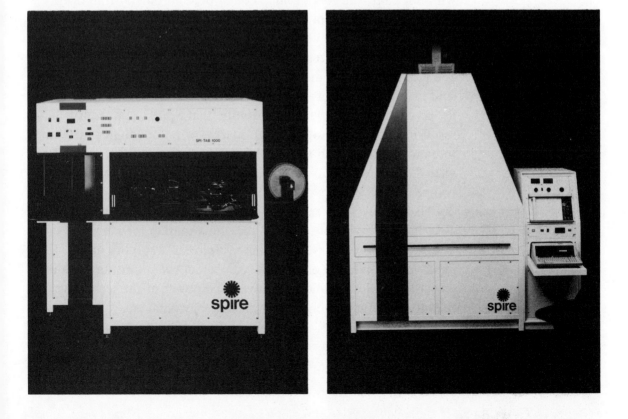

storage system the entire factory could be PV powered as well.

A typical nuclear power plant costs at least $2 billion and requires six to ten years to construct. During that time no power or revenue will be generated but the builder will be paying interest regardless. When the plant is complete, it will generate 500 megawatts. By comparison, the buyer could purchase 80 photovoltaic factories capable of producing 1 megawatt per year for a total investment of less than $150 million—about 6 percent of the nuclear plant's potential cost. The photovoltaic plants would employ about 1000 people, mostly locals, compared with more than 1000 people in design and engineering for six to ten years and then fewer than 200 employees, many nonlocal, after that. The photovoltaic plants could be widely dispersed, minimizing the impact of new technology upon an established culture. Within six months of completion, each plant could begin production of photovoltaic panels—and revenue. In five or six years, the combined production of all the plants would equal or exceed the nuclear plant's potential output, assuming that it was completed.

Critics of Spire's marketing approach are concerned that Spire will "lock up" the foreign market and prevent others from openly competing by developing exclusive agreements with national governments. Others are concerned that the sale of the process machinery will only result in the U.S. "giving away" the photovoltaic industry and the thousands of jobs that might result if we only sold complete products, not factories. Overall, many in the industry perceive a longer term probability, that Spire's approach will result in the flooding of the U.S. market of photovoltaics made in foreign countries with cheaper labor. If this happened it would be virtually impossible for U.S. companies to produce photovoltaics competitively.

The photovoltaic cat is out of the bag and it is highly questionable that any corporation could lock up a market for very long. The very notion that we as a nation, Spire as a corporation, or the photovoltaic industry as a whole can somehow control or limit the technology's development is naive. The power of the technology, literally and figuratively, is too great to be contained.

Conservation and Traveling Light

In 1960 the U.S. population consumed about half the energy, per capita, we used in 1980. As a nation we use anywhere from 150 to 300 percent more electricity than our counterparts in other industrialized countries—Japan, Sweden, England, France, and even Canada. On average our houses are somewhat larger, so we have correspondingly larger lighting and heating demands, but otherwise our lifestyles are not all that different from those of citizens in those countries.

Typically, despite our unbridled consumption habits, when a technology is first introduced we Americans use it reverently, sparingly, as if out of respect for its ability to transform our lives. Undoubtedly there is even some fear of the tool's implications, wise fear, causing us to creep up on it cautiously.

Our approach to electricity reveals this pattern very well. In 1890 we consumed electricity as if it were precious; by 1930 we consumed it carefully but regarded it as commonplace, and by 1970 we had become so accustomed to light-switches and appliances being on we often just left them on.

In 1950, if you looked at a suburban home from the street at night you would have seen only a few 60–100 watt bulbs on—in the kitchen, bathroom, living room or hall. A 25-watt porchlight might have been mesmerizing bugs in the evening but it would have been turned off by midnight. A radio might have been played for thirty minutes, maybe an hour; a desk lamp with a 60-watt bulb might have been on in the den for two or three hours; a refrigerator about two-thirds the size of a 1984 model might have been humming away in the kitchen with its interior stuffed with food—and frost—and in some houses the single TV might have been on for one, or maybe two, hours.

A mere twenty years later, in 1970, you might have passed by the same house, with a new family in residence. From the street you would have seen two exterior spotlights at 100 watts each, one porchlight left on all night long—to drive the local bugs crazy until dead. Inside, in the living room, there would have been two

150-watt three-stage bulbs on at their middle-level illumination. In the kitchen, there would have been a 40-watt fluorescent light over the stove, on, and three incandescent bulbs at 75 watts each recessed in fixtures. Three hall lights, at 50 watts each, a bathroom light at 150 watts, and two bedroom lights at 60 watts each all would have been on. At 7:00 P.M. the dishwasher would have been whirring and one electric burner would have been boiling water for tea. The refrigerator, considerably larger than its predecessor and frost-free, would also have been using electricity, like the freezer in the garage—both on 24 hours a day. The garbage disposal would have been turned on three times a day in separate bursts of high-torque electrical guzzling. Back in one bedroom, one of the kids would have been watching a black-and-white TV while doodling on his homework; out in the living room the rest of the household would have been watching color TV—as they would have done every day for about four hours. They would also have used the stereo system five to eight hours a week. In the garage, a door opener would have been sitting quietly upon its track, awaiting the signal to leap into action.

In 1890 we played with electricity; in 1930 those who had it used it and fantasized about the wondrous technology it might power. In 1970 we were into serious machinery in every house—electrify it all! A chicken in every pot and a plug in every outlet. Burn it up!

Now, in the 1980s, conservation has entered the picture as a theme, creating an odd dichotomy. The corporations that provide electricity are, by necessity, nearly obsessed with efficiency and the minimizing of waste. But for four decades these same corporations advocated increased consumption almost regardless of the implications. They themselves grew more efficient while telling "them"—that is, us—to keep right on wasting. And now, in a turnaround of the general trend, these same utilities, having discovered conservation as a necessary extension of their concern for efficiency, are encouraging us all to conserve.

Many utility companies throughout the United States now offer energy-conservation programs to their customers. In essence these companies have discovered that investing in improving the efficiency of their customer's homes and businesses is equivalent to building a new power plant, but much cheaper and less complex.

As utilities became more conservation oriented, appliance manufacturers, prodded by new government standards, began to build more efficient appliances. Seemingly minor changes in motor design and in control systems have resulted in efficiency improvements of up to 50 percent. A new 1985 refrigerator might use half the energy of the 1970 model of the same size. Heating and air conditioning units have benefited from a high degree of research into all facets of energy consumption and the movement of energy in our world.

For example, the simple heat pump can typically operate by the differential between the Earth's almost constant temperature of 50 to 60 degrees and the atmospheric temperature, which can be much higher, or lower, than the Earth's temperature. Such apparently minor "technical fixes" are now integrated into thousands of consumer products. While they may seem inconsequential individually, if much of the U.S. population rapidly shifted over to the more efficient appliances while simultaneously using lighting more carefully, these innovations could result in a dramatic drop in electrical consumption.

From the homeowner's point of view, the steps needed to conserve heating energy, decrease electrical consumption, and increasingly solarize a home are best taken one at a time. It is possible to do it all at once, but it is easier and more practical to take each step as a small project for a few weekend afternoons. The necessary changes are of two sorts: material—installing weatherstripping and insulation—and behavioral—making sure the newly weatherstripped windows are kept closed at the right times, for instance, and consistently paying attention to the wattage of bulbs and the efficiency of appliances.

However, the value of conservation in the home is not merely the reduction of our heating and electrical bills. Those costs are embodied in the products and services we buy, and we, as individuals, are economically just as pressed to maximize efficiency within the household as any large corporation. While our "profits" as householders may not show on an annual report balance sheet, they are nonetheless a factor in maintaining a home budget in the black. The more efficient our homes are the less reliant we are upon economic forces over which we have no control.

While it may be tempting to dismiss conservation at a time when oil prices are stable, or declining, it must be recognized that those of us living in industrialized countries, unlike our counterparts in underdeveloped regions, are reliant upon an extraordinarily complex array of technological devices, most of which require electricity. We may think of these things as conveniences, but if we equate each convenience with the hours worked to buy and power that convenience, then the word *convenient* takes on quite another meaning. In this context, conservation need not be thought of as a moral imperative but as a means of decreasing the number of hours worked to use a convenience.

The American Home Market

In America in the 1980s electricity is regarded as just short of a right. Government regulatory agencies force utilities to provide "lifeline," or minimal rates, to the poor. Welfare agencies consider electricity to be as crucial as basic foodstuffs. To most Americans, the very idea of being cold in the dark is not just a normal fear but a thought of terrifying implications. In a single century, we have totally integrated cheap and available energy into our way of life and view of reality. We've gone from trying to keep warm in dim light and accepting those conditions as normal to being nearly terrified at the prospect of lower than "normal" temperatures in anything less than a few hundred watts of light.

We are still capable of living without electricity. However, with the loss of electricity, our civilization would be so radically altered so fast that it is hard to imagine what life might be like ten years after it occurred. So the fear of being without electricity is not without sense; it is really the fear of losing our gains as a culture and species. Electricity, even more than money, is the single most critical element in the truest improvement we have made in the quality of our lives.

Now, for the first time since the widespread application of electricity, we have the opportunity to radically alter the way electricity is generated, where it is generated, how much is generated, and how we pay for its generation. Photovoltaics can radically simplify the process of generation, they can be deployed in practically any imaginable format, their system size can be precisely matched to specific needs, and they can be purchased on a one-time basis, just as one might buy a new roof.

The ways to electrify a house with photovoltaics are as varied as houses themselves and the circumstances in which they exist. A first step might be to install a "security system" involving a small outside light and built-in photovoltaic module. A small exterior system might cost between $50 and $500. Another small system might power five lightbulbs and a television set in a garage converted into an apartment. A larger system would power a vacation

A 100-percent solar home near Borrego Springs in the Southern California desert southeast of Los Angeles. The home is powered by eighteen 35-watt ARCO solar PV panels, visible at left. The system puts out about 600 watts of peak power, or 3.5 kilowatt hours per day. The home is about 1400 square feet in area and receives all its energy, including space and water heating, from the sun. Back-up heating is by gas and woodstove. The PV panels powered many of the construction tools used in building the house. The home was built in 1982.

(Source: Borrego Solar Systems)

home, small cabin or recreation vehicle—five to ten modules with a bank of batteries would power a 12-volt lighting and refrigeration system. Small houses or small apartments with three to five rooms and modest energy requirements could be electrified with a few modules and a battery bank. Larger houses, apartment buildings, and commercial buildings could utilize systems tied to the utility grid so they generate power for the structure or pump power into the utility grid; alternately, the utility tie could serve as a back-up source of electricity only. Or the system could stand alone, with battery storage only and no utility connection at all.

Complexes of apartments and clusters of houses in some neighborhoods might require concentrating or tracking photovoltaic systems located within the complex or nearby where maximum sunlight is available. Whole city blocks, or communities of ten to twenty blocks, might develop neighborhood-scaled photovoltaic plants to provide electricity and hot water. Above the neighborhood scale, photovoltaic plants built by utilities or private entrepreneurs could be installed atop all manner of structure, in open

fields, along power-line rights of way, and in countless forgotten corners of property within any city.

Electricity can be generated and transmitted either as direct or alternating current—that is, dc or ac. Conventional generating stations provide electricity that is alternating, ac, at the point of use; 110 or 220 volts ac is typical home-outlet power. Photovoltaic cells inherently produce direct current. Therefore, electrifying a typical American home with photovoltaics requires the conversion, through what is called an inverter, of dc to ac. Alternatively, one can rewire all circuits and purchase appliances that only accept 12 volts dc. Twelve-volt dc systems and appliances are relatively common in boats, recreation vehicles, and vacation cabins. All the necessary technology is available and proven—see your local RV and marine supply dealers in the yellow pages. Converting to 12-volt power is probably not an option for most of us, however. The much simpler route is to convert photovoltaic-generated electricity to ac.

A power-conditioning unit, which often includes an inverter, is

An adobe home in Santa Fe, New Mexico. The roof-mounted PV array produces 3 kilowatts of electricity. The home is all-solar, including a solar greenhouse, domestic water heating, solar space heating and even a solar-heated hot tub. This house was originally built as a demonstration project. When it went on the market it was purchased within 24 hours.

(Source: Steven J. Strong, Solar Design Associates)

an innocuous-looking box about the size of a stereo speaker. This unit must do three things: invert the power from dc to ac; maintain the wave form of outgoing electricity so that it matches the waves of incoming utility power for which appliances are designed; and ensure that sufficient power is provided steadily, regardless of the fluctuating output of photovoltaics. The sun passing behind a cloud can suddenly cause a drop in photovoltaic output. The conditioning unit senses the decline and automatically makes up for the loss from utility sources or batteries. If there is not enough power available from batteries, the conditioning unit's circuit breakers will break the circuit, preventing damage to appliances on the line.

The three basic types of building-mounted photovoltaic power systems. (a) A typical array that could be placed atop a building or on the ground near the building. (b) The range of typical appliances that could be powered. (c) Three system variations. (d) A power-conditioning and inverter unit tied to the utility meter. When the PV system is generating electricity, it powers the house directly, but when power output falls off during cloudy weather or at night, the utility system is automatically activated to provide back-up power. (e) A utility-intertied system that allows the PV system to power the house and generate power back into the utility grid when the house does not need the PV system's peak output—usually at midday. (f) An inverter and battery system with no connection to the utility grid.

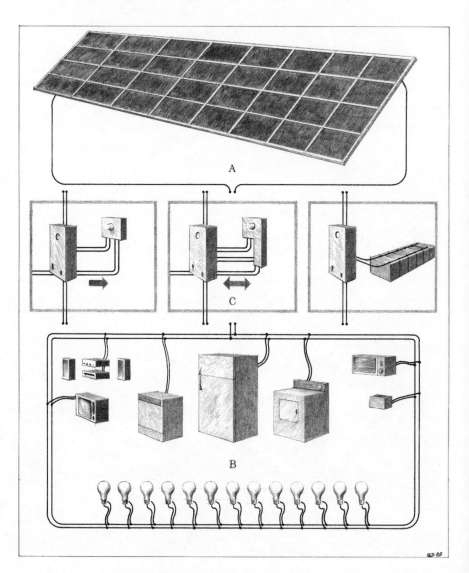

Similarly, if too many appliances are on-line and turned on, over-loading the system's capacity, the power-conditioning unit will break the circuit and prevent damage to the PV modules.

Sizing a photovoltaic system, and particularly the power-conditioning unit, requires the estimating of the system's total wattage—the sum of all appliances that might be drawing upon the system at any given moment—and the "surge" loads that will occur when a motor starts. It is to this surge load that the conditioning unit responds in preventing the overloading of the system's components. A wide range of power-conditioning units, at many different scales, are now available. While research into power conditioners has not received the attention that PV cells have, it is highly probable that expanded PV sales will result in cheaper power-conditioning units as well as additional research.

In 1943, the typical American submarine on patrol in the Pacific used deep-cycle electric batteries when it submerged. When the ship was on the surface, its diesel engine would drive the ship while charging the batteries. Essentially, the same type of deep-cycle batteries are now sold for recreation vehicles, boats, small power plants where substantial storage capacity is needed, and houses. Similar batteries are also used in golf carts and forklift trucks. Although they look like automotive batteries and function much like them, the deep-cycle battery is capable of being almost totally drained, and it can be totally recharged hundreds of times before it wears out. An automobile battery is not designed for a total drain-recharge cycle. When such a battery is down after the car is started, the alternator charges it back up again so it is always nearly fully charged.

Existing photovoltaic systems in mountain cabins, as well as many larger systems built to power public or commercial buildings, contain a rack of batteries—from two or three up to fifty or more—capable of storing sufficient power to sustain the building's operation for a few weeks without direct sun. Battery systems now in use represent a very high level of battery technology. The industry has been making steady improvements since well before World War II. Although deep-cycle batteries are heavy and awkward to move, they are otherwise very simple, straightforward, reliable, and durable. Depending on the use cycles—the pattern of charge and discharge—of a given system, plus air temperature and type of batteries, a typical storage system can be cycled from a few

A typical deep-cycle battery used to store electricity at night and during cloudy periods. Although closely related to the automotive battery, deep-cycle batteries are designed to be totally, or almost totally, discharged and then recharged. This battery is made by Surrette Battery, which once built batteries for diesel-electric submarines in WWII.

(Source: Surrette Battery Company)

hundred to more than 1500 times before the batteries will need to be replaced. Batteries can last from four to eight years, maybe ten.

The elements of the system, then, are photovoltaics on the roof, inverter in a corner of the garage, and possibly batteries in another corner behind a safe enclosure.

Sizing a system begins with a thorough inventory of the building's electrical needs. From the inventory, you can generate a shopping list of options. Once the options are clear, you'll need to understand the relationship of the sun to the house—how many hours per day at all times of the year the house is clearly receiving sun, and where on the roof, or within the property line, the sunlight is most heavily concentrated. In addition, it will be necessary to check local and regional weather maps to determine approximately how many full-sun days are likely to occur within a given year as well as how much sunlight is received in the area, on average, every year. Merging information about the home and its occu-

The pattern of sunlight over the entire planet. Some areas receive far more sun than others. In designing a PV system, one must consult references on the sunlight available in a given area. The lighter, generally desert areas of the map receive the most sun and the darker cold areas the least. Since most of the world's population resides in temperature zones with more than adequate sunlight, PVs are widely applicable.

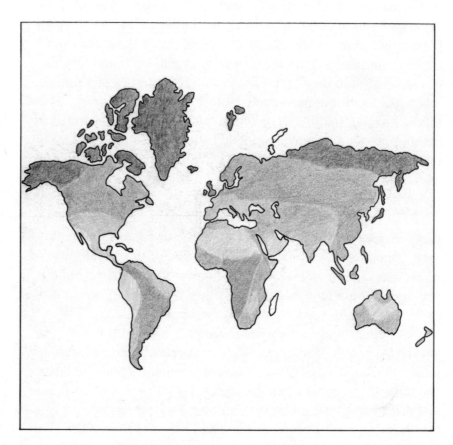

pants' needs with information about the sun's position during various periods of the year will yield an impression of the relationship between incoming sunlight and the occupants' electrical demands.

Once the system is approximately sized relative to input and necessary output, then you can begin to make choices about the type of system to be installed—that is, grid-tied, grid back-up only, or stand-alone.

Owing to regulatory changes mandated by PURPA, it is currently possible for a homeowner to build a photovoltaic system and then to pump power back into the utility grid—virtually causing the meter to run backwards—when the homeowner is not utilizing the system's output. In effect the home system becomes an independent power plant paid for by the excess energy it produces. However, the required electrical connections, including a more complex power-conditioning unit than usual, often make this option a dubious financial gain. Furthermore, uncertainties surrounding the utility's acceptance of the power remain, since utility policies do not always favor independent power producers, despite the change in regulations. Still, if the house and its PV system is large enough, a surplus of power will easily be produced. Utility-tied systems are quite feasible and, in terms of installation at least, are the cheapest of the photovoltaic systems. No batteries are required and one has the best of both worlds, plus a check whenever the system generates utility power. But if the utility grid blacks out. . .

The second possibility eliminates the problems of conditioning and metering power back to the utility. The utility connection is maintained as back-up power only, with perhaps a small bank of batteries for storage in case the utility power goes out. This is certainly a workable approach, but it would portend an eventual decline in utility service if it became widespread. If more than 30 percent of the homes and commercial structures in a given area came to depend on the utility only for an occasional shot of juice when their PV systems were not producing, the burden of maintaining the utility line would fall upon all other users. The utility would be forced either to raise prices for its customers in that area or to assume a loss on the line. Obviously, over a period of years such a pattern would erode the utility's entire rate base. The result: higher prices for the remaining users, which could, in turn, force more people to convert to photovoltaics—which of course would

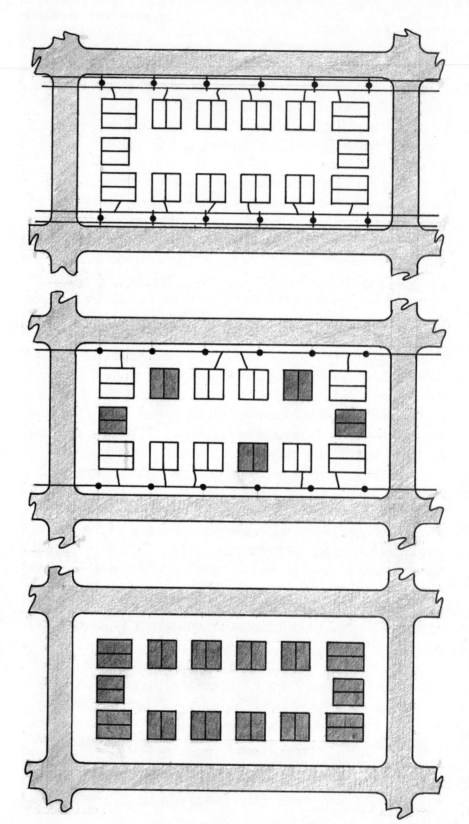

A guess as to how photovoltaic technology will spread and the degree to which it will become a standard material on house roofs. A few houses with PV systems, some independent and some tied to utility grids, will initiate the change. Finally, over a period of decades, the grid will become uneconomical. This scenario assumes that battery-storage technology will become cheaper, both initially and in replacement cost, than maintaining the grid.

only further erode the rate base.

The third possibility by-passes the utility entirely. The photo-voltaics are used to continually charge a bank of batteries that have sufficient capacity to carry the house through long periods—possibly up to three weeks—without any direct sun under overcast skies. However, this estimate of battery-storage capacity assumes that no electrical heating is used. A stand-alone system is not a good idea in an electrically heated home since electric heaters devour electricity, and are often used for many hours at a time. Electric stoves and ovens, on the other hand, tend to be far more concentrated; they are inherently more efficient than heaters and they are only used for short periods of time, so they work well with stand-alone systems.

How these three basic systems develop and how they will perform in relation to utility companies remains to be seen. The large spread in system costs, with utility-tied systems tending to be cheaper than stand-alone systems, may diminish. Power conditioning and battery costs may drop as a direct result of mass production for photovoltaic applications. And utility companies may or may not favor intertied systems involving hundreds, or possibly thousands, of independent producers. Indeed, the development of lower cost photovoltaic systems for houses will raise a raft of

Home Photovoltaic-System Costs, 1984–1995

System Parts	1984	1995
Photovoltaic module/panel per peak watt	$8–12	$.25–.40
Mounting hardware	1–2	.05–.10
Batteries	1–6	.75–4
Voltage regulator	.50–3	.15–.50
Inverter (converts DC to AC)	1–5	.25–.50
Wiring and installation	1–7	.40–.70

Total costs for 5000-watt (5-kilowatt) system

	1984	1995
Totally independent system, low	$ 62,500	$ 9,250
Totally independent system, high	175,000	31,000
Utility-intertied (no batteries) system, low	55,000	4,750
Utility-intertied system, high	130,000	8,500

Note: Projected 1995 prices are based on a combination of industry forecasts and intuitive assumptions. It is generally assumed that price reduction will occur through increased volume, production efficiencies, product innovations, and familiarity with installation.

issues with respect to utilities, issues that will no doubt come to the fore in countless policy discussions inside and outside the utility companies.

Environmental and regional considerations will also have their impact on system design. There are countless apartment buildings, multiple-unit houses, clusters of houses, and whole neighborhoods whose density of electrical demand exceeds what could be provided by rooftop photovoltaics alone. The limitation might be regional climate—long foggy periods, for example—the location of the buildings relative to a north slope, the presence of forest, or even towering nearby buildings shading the structures. Whatever the specific circumstances, we are sure to see the development of photovoltaic systems designed to meet such needs. The roof of an apartment building might include a cogenerating concentrating module like the unit now produced by United Energy Corporation or Entech of Dallas, Texas. Such a unit would recharge the building's battery-storage system while providing hot water for building heat and water. Perhaps an entire city block composed of two- and three-story apartments in row houses would join together to purchase a cluster of concentrating modules located on the roofs of the particular buildings that received the most sun.

In most instances where photovoltaics might be used, modules could be placed on an existing or slightly modified roof. Concentrating cogeneration units providing hot water and electricity are usually larger and more substantial than standard units and require some additional support to distribute their weight on a flat roof. But overall PV units are not particularly heavy, so no major structural support changes would be required on most buildings.

The optimum position for modules in much of the continental United States is facing south with the modules elevated slightly— 20 to 30 degrees. This position ensures that a maximum amount of southern winter sun strikes the modules. Obviously, the best circumstance is a clear unshaded roof, preferably the longest panel of roof on the building, sloped at about 30 degrees with the peak of the roof running east to west. Unfortunately, relatively few buildings are so optimally sited. In most instances, the building will not be perfectly oriented and the PV modules will require placement on one end of the roof, or upon a built-up framework.

Photovoltaic modules can be easily installed on a built-up wood or metal framework set off a roof or perhaps forming part of a trel-

Mounting photovoltaic modules. (a) On flat roofs or in open stand-alone applications apart from a building, a simple wood, aluminum, or steel frame can be built to angle the modules to the south. (b) Small arrays integrated with a trellis. The possibilities in integrating PV panels into all manner of exterior garden structures are practically endless. (c) A light metal frame supporting PV modules over a conventional shingle roof. This method is quite workable but must be used with care to minimize moisture problems in roofing under modules. (d) PV modules mounted directly on the roof, or set into the existing roof and caulked. (e) Large-area modules of polycrystalline or amorphous silicon. These panels can be installed as one would install any roofing material. (f) Glass roofing tiles laid atop a plywood subroof, the ultimate modular electric roofing material.

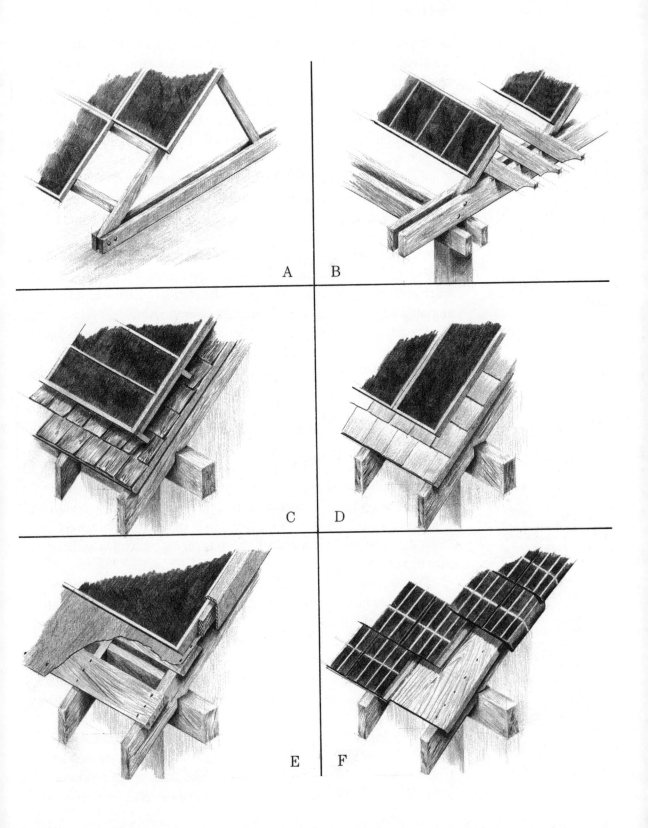

A

B

C

D

E

F

lis or porch roof. It is also possible to integrate the PV installation with various changes in the home's form to maximize solar gain for heating. Typically, the conversion of an existing home to solar almost always requires the addition or expansion of south-facing glass in the form of windows, sliding glass doors, a greenhouse, and/or skylights. The installation of photovoltaics can be included in such a conversion.

Photovoltaic modules can also be simply attached directly to the roof with a light wooden frame to prevent moisture from collecting beneath the modules and rotting or otherwise damaging the roofing material. An alternate strategy might involve removing a portion of the roofing material and setting the modules into the roof so that they become an integral component. This would minimize moisture problems and reduce the roof's overall weight, important if snow and ice loads are a consideration.

Clearly the best approach to installing photovoltaics is to install modules *as* the roofing material. New solar homes, such as the Carlisle house near Boston, which was one of the first 100 percent solar homes, are almost entirely roofed with photovoltaics. The modules become large sheets of roofing material, analogous to plywood sheets, and can be installed with practically the same techniques. If ARCO Solar modules were used to totally roof a typical house, they'd easily generate an excess of power. Slightly less efficient—and less expensive—polycrystalline cells or ribbon cells would be even more economical as a full-roof installation. Various research efforts aimed at producing large-area cells are now yielding a low-cost roofing material in the form of amorphous silicon film bonded to a glass substrate.

Without doubt, the most exciting product to evolve from PV research to date is a simple roofing tile. In 1983, Sanyo of Japan, in cooperation with Ashai Glass Company, announced it had developed such a product. Westinghouse has shown strong interest in developing a similar product. The Sanyo product, called "Amorton Tile," is a glass tile thinly coated with amorphous silicon material. The company has announced that the product will be on the market in 1985 or 1986.

Replacing a roof is a periodic expenditure that comes with owning a building. The cost for a typical house might be anywhere from $10,000 to more than $25,000. If the roof were composed of glass tiles, glass being one of the hardest materials known, it

Tracking photovoltaic systems, either single- or double-axis in operation. The perspective view of the basic mechanical function of a two-axis tracking system (a) reveals how elementary the concept is. Motors are geared to the vertical and horizontal shafts. Double-axis trackers can follow the sun daily and seasonally, always remaining precisely focused perpendicular to the sun's rays. (b) Single axis is less efficient in winter, since it cannot angle south.

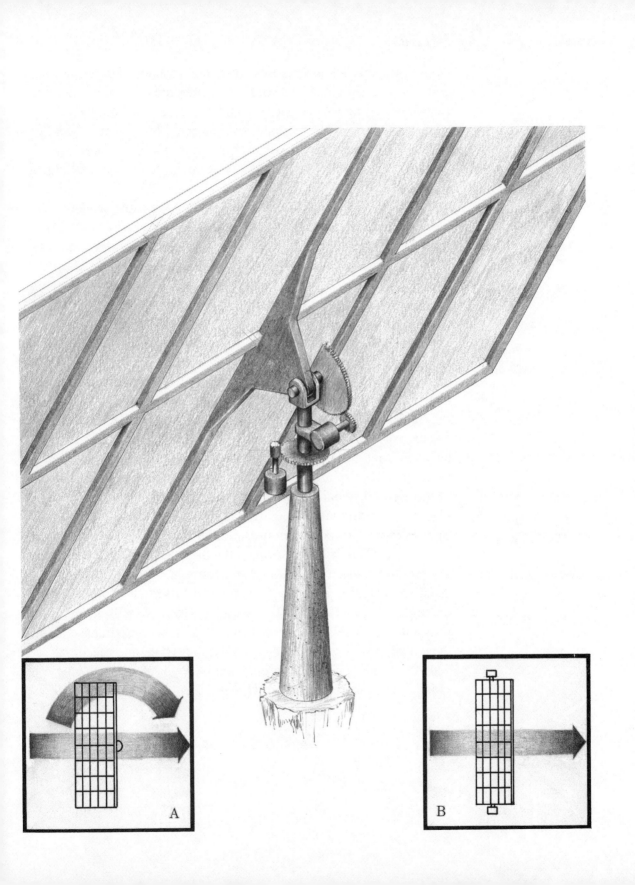

would probably last longer than comparable wood shingle, terra cotta tile, or asphalt. If the roof also generated electricity, then the cost of installing a PV system would decrease since the PVs on the roof would be solving two problems at once. Moreover, since the homeowner would have to replace the roof anyway, making the changes necessary to install a photovoltaic system would be highly cost beneficial.

Though hard, glass is a brittle material. Repeated sandstorms blowing across a piece of tempered window glass will eventually scratch the surface and frost the glass. But it takes many years of such wear before the glass loses an appreciable degree of clarity. Glass covers single- or polycrystal photovoltaic modules protecting the cells from damage, similarly a thin glass coating can be placed over amorphous cells to protect the thin silicon coating from damage and roof tiles made of glass would have to withstand the onslaught of heavy rains, sleet, hail, snow and ice formation. Experience to date with a variety of photovoltaic modules indicates that glass used to protect them can easily withstand all but the very rare hailstorm with golf-ball sized hailstones, and even that may not damage all the modules on a typical roof. The failures that have occurred have mostly been due to rain or ice finding a crack in the module's framing where it meets the glass, and such failures of more recently built modules are relatively rare.

The uncertainties surrounding the photovoltaic industry to date, especially with respect to homebuilding, have been made abundantly clear. But one fact seems obvious—the idea of a roofing tile capable of generating electricity is almost as startling and wondrous an invention as the photovoltaic cell itself. It is probably inevitable that in 1991, 1993, or maybe 1995, we will be able to walk into our local home-improvement centers and purchase cartons of roofing tiles that will transform our roofs into electrical generators. Perhaps the only question is, Will the product say "Made in Japan" or "Made in U.S.A."?

Portentous Markets: Railroads, Mormons, and Australians

Those who market photovoltaics, like anyone marketing a new product, must be concerned with all the usual factors—price, dependability, service—but because of the product's widespread applicability they are also concerned with another factor: the implications of selling photovoltaics to a particular customer in a particular place. Selling photovoltaics to China is perhaps the most dramatic example of a sale with overwhelming implications.

Railroads and pipeline companies are known for their conservatism when it comes to new technology. They cannot afford failures. They are nearly obsessed with reliability. Burlington Northern Railroad, one of the most progressive railroads in the business, has trackage across much of the northwestern United States. It is not uncommon to find grade crossings, signals, and related technology located out in the middle of nowhere—miles from the nearest utility line.

The Alaska Railroad, between Fairbanks and Anchorage, has similarly remote needs. The Alaska Railroad recently installed photovoltaic-powered repeaters for its radio communication system, and Burlington Northern, in only the last few years, has installed more than 300 photovoltaic systems. In most cases these installations have replaced battery-powered systems or eliminated the need of new power lines.

One railroad or one pipeline company purchasing photovoltaics and installing them in a variety of applications speaks to the larger world of basic industries. Through articles in the trade press, practically all North American railroad-management people concerned with remote-site power problems are now aware of Burlington Northern's success. Inevitably, other companies will follow the lead, and indications are that this is already happening. For example, another large western railroad is now planning to electrify some of its remote maintenance buildings with PVs. As activity increases, new applications will become larger and more visible.

There are also large groups of people who, like specific industries, have unusual needs and concerns. Utah is heavily populated by members of the Mormon faith. Characteristically, Mormons have an unusually acute concern for their survival in the face of horrific famines, diseases, and wars. Many Mormon families, as an article of faith, maintain substantial stocks of canned goods and bulk foodstuffs of all kinds as insurance against disaster. Consistent with their philosophy, many Mormon families also maintain small generators and gas supplies that would provide them with a modest amount of electricity during a disaster.

It is conceivable that Mormons could become a major primary market for home-mounted photovoltaic systems, predominantly stand-alone systems with no electrical connection to utilities. Not only would photovoltaics allow a Mormon family to remain electrified throughout all but the most total disaster—that is, nuclear war and its subsequent winter—but the very existence of a PV system would be a dramatic statement of the church's uncommon emphasis on self-reliance and the values of the home.

Australia remains something of an anomaly among industrialized Western nations. It is as highly advanced, both culturally and industrially, as any country on the planet, but it lacks the kind of

A Kansas City Southern freight about to clear a block signal near Hume, Kansas. The signals, and a track circuit that triggers the transition from red to green, are powered by a NiCad battery recharged by 20 watts of photovoltaic modules atop the stand in the foreground.

(Source: ARCO Solar)

thorough grid system we in the United States take for granted. Utility-generated power is accessible around practically all of Australia's major cities on the east and west coasts, but in between it is practically unheard of. Development in Australia's outback is limited by the availability of two basics: water and power. Where electricity does exist, much of it ends up being used to pump up water from deep wells. If well water is unavailable or too deep, then one uses a cistern to store rainwater. In either case, diesel-electric generators are the critical basic element in developing a ranch, "station," or small town.

There might not be much water in the middle of Australia's vast outback, or even in many areas of its pristine coastline, but there is more than enough sun. Australia has sun, sun, and more sun: it is drenched in sun. Predictably, therefore, research and development work towards the creation of an Australian photovoltaic industry is well underway. As in many Third World countries, the electrification of Australian outback settlements is a question of high-priced, troublesome, and fuel-dependent diesel-generated electricity; photovoltaic-generated electricity; maybe a wind gener-

Tideland Signal Corporation specializes in photovoltaic powered navigation aids. Here a technician checks the inner workings of a navigation light. The plastic-encased photovoltaics are an integral part of the entire product. The use of photovoltaics in such an unforgiving environment, and for a purpose so vital to the safety of people, is a testament to the technology's dependability.

(Source: Tideland Signal Corporation)

ator; or no electricity at all. Given the long distances a truck must travel to carry diesel fuel and gasoline to remote points, and the inevitable higher costs that result, photovoltaic cells would appear to be a heavenly deal. Photovoltaics will no doubt become very, very common in Australia.

For obvious reasons, photovoltaic technology in Australia is a natural. Less obvious are the implications of widespread PV development in such an arid place. Although it is too early to detect any trends beyond the mere existence of a fledgling Australian PV industry, it is highly probable that cheaper PV systems than those existing now will allow, to some extent, the development of remote areas of Australian outback. That may not necessarily have entirely positive ramifications; in fact, it may have very negative environmental ramifications. We shall see.

The full range of Tideland Signal Corporation's navigational aids, most of which are PV powered, or can be. The three white boxes with PV cells atop are portable solar generators, with batteries for long-term storage of electricity.

(Source: Tideland Signal Corporation)

The Great Utility Market

When presented with a magnifying glass on a sunny day, the average eight-year-old boy soon learns the power of the sun, though, it is hoped, not on his skin. Invariably he finds the right combination of alignment with the sun and focus of the glass. He often comes to this discovery using a leaf or candy wrapper, which of course is consumed in flame once the temperature reaches ignition. A magnifying glass merely concentrates the sun's light on a tiny pinpoint. Heat is the result.

Photographs of distant stars barely discernible to the naked eye are taken with slow camera exposures that allow the film to absorb points of light not visible at all, even by a trained eye. Accomplishing this apparently simple act requires a complex of gears, motors, and computer-control systems that slowly and very, very accurately move the telescope to compensate for the Earth's movement in relation to the star, or stars, being photographed. The telescope must be moved on two axes, north to south and east to west, simultaneously.

On the same principle as both the examples, photovoltaics can be made to track the sun for the maximal gathering of power. Four utility-scale 1-megawatt-plus photovoltaic power plants have now been built in California, and all employ tracking methods. The Sacramento Municipal Utility District's 2-megawatt plant near Sacramento uses "off-the-shelf" photovoltaic modules placed in arrays that track the sun from east to west, morning to dusk. Since the modules only move in one plane, east to west, they are known as single-axis trackers. ARCO Solar's Lugo Station power plant east of Los Angeles is approximately the same size as the Sacramento facility, but it utilizes large square arrays, composed of off-the-shelf modules, mounted on double-axis tracking mechanisms. Lugo Station not only tracks east to west from sunup to sundown, but its panels automatically adjust to the sun's gradual movement north to south, summer to winter. Double-axis trackers are always in the optimum position perpendicular to the sun's rays.

North of Los Angeles on a dry plain sits a third utility-scale facility, built for Pacific Gas & Electric, a San Francisco-based utility. Like Lugo Station it uses double-axis trackers, but in addition to the conventional ARCO Solar modules, each panel includes winglike mirrors that bounce additional light onto the cells, further increasing efficiency. And northeast of Los Angeles in the desert near Barstow, California, is an energy "farm" built by United Energy Corporation and now selling electricity to Southern California Edison. The farm's fields are large round ponds, each containing numerous floating photovoltaic concentrating and tracking units. The concentrating system uses fresnel lenses—ribbed plastic sheets consisting of hundreds of concentric linear "lenses"—to focus sunlight upon photovoltaic cells barely a half inch in diameter. The heat generated by the intensely concentrated sunlight is drawn off by water-filled copper tubes located just behind the cell. The entire photovoltaic array sits upon a frame equipped with small motors that cause the modules and the entire array to move every few minutes to follow the sun. The hot water is later used as a primary energy source in a nearby ethanol distillery, also being constructed by United Energy Corporation.

Detail of the Sacramento Municipal Utility District's PV plant. The panels are composed of ARCO Solar off-the-shelf modules. Small motors at the top of each stanchion are visible. The motors gradually turn the PVs as the sun moves across the sky. The plant's stark look and elegant simplicity are startling on first sight.

(Source: Sacramento Municipal Utility District)

A single-axis tracking system that follows the sun from east to west can increase the output of typical modules by 20 to 30 percent. Double-axis tracking systems can increase output by up to 50 percent, and concentrators can increase both the efficiency of the cells themselves and their potential output owing to their perfect orientation toward the sun. Concentrators have another benefit—they are cogenerating units that can provide a substantial amount of heat in the form of hot water. If both the electricity and hot water are translated into common energy units, the efficiency of a typical unit can top 60 percent.

The quantity of energy required to steadily move photovoltaic panels represents only a fraction of the whole system's output. Clearly, the added complexity of tracking and the power it requires is far outweighed by the gains in system output. And this remains true even if the system is relatively small, so there is no necessary economy of scale implied by tracking and concentrating systems.

The four photovoltaic plants now in operation in California clearly demonstrate the feasibility of the technology on the utility scale. There is no doubt we will see the development of other

An "energy farm" built by the United Energy Corporation in Southern California's Mojave Desert. PV modules float on the round ponds generating electricity and hot water. The latter is used in distilling feedstock into ethanol at a nearby UEC plant. The electricity is sold to the regional utility.

(Source: United Energy Corporation)

utility-scale photovoltaic facilities, but it remains to be seen which technologies will be used under what circumstances and on what scales. However, one trend appears to be emerging already, and that involves the use of cogenerating modules in industrial applications where both electricity and hot water are needed.

Although tax-credit-assisted financing has been a critical ingredient in the economic equation of such plants to date, it is likely that the high efficiency of these installations—with electricity and

Pacific Gas & Electric's photovoltaic facility northwest of Los Angeles. The mirror at left increases the amount of sunlight hitting the cells, in this case ARCO modules. This is a "semi-concentrator" tracking system.

(Source: ARCO Solar)

hot water being produced by the same module—will result in their economical use sooner than simple tracking units generating electricity alone. Photovoltaic cogeneration systems are a natural for municipal and emergency facilities where on-site dependable power is needed in the event of a disaster. Cogeneration systems could provide emergency power—with a bank of batteries—and hot water for space heat.

Southern California Edison, SCE, is the dominant utility in Southern California. SCE supplies more than 3.5 billion dollars of electricity to its southern California and Los Angeles basin customers every year. As described in an earlier section, it buys power from a broad range of generating technologies, including oil- or natural-gas fired steam-generating stations, hydroelectric, nuclear, geothermal, wind, cogeneration (conventional cogeneration systems involve a diesel engine driving a generator with waste engine heat used to heat water), solar thermal, and most recently photovoltaics. SCE operates in a region famous for its freeways and the most noxious cloud of air pollution on the North American continent. SCE's system serves lonely desert outposts where the line

Pacific Gas & Electric's photovoltaic facility from the air. Note the small buildings within the field. Inside are the various switches and power-conditioning units. Coming upon this place unexpectedly is a surreal experience.

(Source: ARCO Solar)

poles are filled with woodpecker holes; it serves research teams at places like the Jet Propulsion Laboratory in Pasadena, where photovoltaic research goes on next door to interplanetary probe design. It serves Atlantic Richfield's main offices in downtown Los Angeles, movie star homes in Malibu and Topanga, and oil pump motors behind a Burger King in El Segundo. Given the diversity within its service region, and the often bizarre habits of those who live there, it is perhaps fitting that SCE was the first utility to seriously shift towards a policy of renewable development only: it will build no more coal, oil, natural-gas, or nuclear facilities.

Forbes magazine's April 27, 1981, issue carried an article about Southern California Edison and its then recent policy shift. The subtitle of the article was, "When was the last time you heard from an enthusiastic utility executive?" In somewhat glowing terms, the article outlined the utility's new direction as a visionary move with far-reaching implications. In the fall of 1980, SCE management had been faced with the need to expand the system's capacity by 6,000 megawatts above the system's current peak load capacity of 15,000 megawatts, a 33 percent increase in the 1980s

The first utility-scale photovoltaic plant in the world, Lugo Station near San Bernardino, California. The plant generates 1 megawatt, was built in an unprecedented 38 weeks, and has been operating nonstop since 1983 with practically no problems.

(Source: Southern California Edison)

and early 90s. Effectively, the choices were coal, more nuclear, new oil plants, possibly hydroelectric, diesel cogeneration, conservation, geothermal, wind, solar thermal, and photovoltaics. The decision included conservation, solar thermal, diesel cogeneration, nuclear from a plant now coming on-line, geothermal, wind, and photovoltaic. SCE was to be involved in a jointly owned coal-fired facility, but they dropped out of the project soon after determining the need of a new strategy.

Large-scale utility generating plants take years to build. Utilities, by necessity, have become accustomed to long-term planning and making decisions—based on hunches as much as reliable engineering research—that they may be living with five or ten years down the road whether they like it or not. In the first months of 1982, ARCO Solar agreed to build and operate a 1-megawatt photovoltaic facility east of San Bernardino supplying power into the Southern California Edison grid. After 38 weeks of construction Lugo Station was built and operating. By the end of 1982, SCE had an additional 1-megawatt power plant operating at better than 92 percent reliability. Lugo Station is still on, day in and day out.

The starkly simple Lugo Station. The elegant design is particularly notable when one considers that most of the structural support for the PV panels, barely visible in this shot of a single tracking unit, is composed of simple off-the-shelf industrial trusses. Compared to most highly sophisticated utility plants, Lugo Station is basic hardware-store engineering.

(Source: Southern California Edison)

The plant is on the high desert near San Bernardino. Inside a fenced square set out on a plain covered with dry scrub the land is bared smooth and flat. At precise intervals, in staggered rows, stand billboard-sized panels mounted on short steel piers set in concrete. The panels tilt steeply towards the morning sun as it rises at the horizon line. The pink morning light bathes the blackish purple face of the crystal modules in a translucent glow. A barely perceptible hum can be heard from the small motors, which move the 108 panels very slowly in the start of their day's journey following the sun across the desert sky.

At noon, the sun is straight overhead and only the seriously deranged would walk out there in the scrub. The panels stand like 108 square umbrellas casting perfectly square shadows—on the right day of the year it looks like a chessboard out there. In the center of the field sits a squat steel building of pure no-nonsense design. In it is a system of switches, meters, and power conditioners that hum in the cooled interior. The building's skin is skillet hot. At the edge of the field a tuned ear on a dry day can hear the high-tension lines buzzing with electrons.

Dusk, and the last light seems to be lost on the panels as they become black. It goes like that every day, again and again, with no one to see it happen except the jackrabbits and occasional visitor or maintenance person. No one stays with the plant like a boilerman would babysit burners.

Each of the 108 panels is composed of 256 photovoltaic modules, 12 by 48 inches in size and rated at 35 to 43 watts. Each module contains 36 silicon wafers encased within a glass and aluminum frame. Each panel carries 9,216 solar cells—the total in 108 panels is 995,328 cells. Like leaves absorbing the energy of the sun and passing it to the tree, the individual cells transform the sun's rays into electrical energy, which is passed from cell to module, to panel, to inverters—changing it from direct into alternating current—to transformers, to high-tension wires, and finally to customers.

North of Lugo Station in the desert near Barstow, California, stands Solar One, another solar generating station built under Department of Energy grants to provide power to Southern California Edison. Although it is a solar-thermal not photovoltaic facility, Solar One could one day result in a merging of two technologies—solar-thermal and photovoltaics. The station is a central tower surrounded by a field of 1,818 mirrors—heliostats. The mirrors, which utilize a tracking system very similar to that of Lugo Station, follow the sun throughout the day. At the center of the field of mirrors stands a tower with a ceramic cap containing a working fluid. The mirrors focus sunlight upon the ceramic surface until it turns nearly white hot. The fluid, heated to a high temperature, is circulated through a series of heat-exchanging tubes in which the heat is transferred to water, which turns to steam and is piped to turbines. The turbines drive generators. Unlike the photovoltaic facility, which has no storage capability, Solar One is capable of storing a portion of the heat generated during the day in underground heat-storage chambers. The heat can then be released at a controlled rate during the evening to generate additional power.

Farther east in the Mojave Desert another solar-thermal plant is now in operation. Instead of a central tower, this facility uses parabolic troughs, long dish-shaped panels finished like mirrors, with tubes carrying a working fluid located at the center of the trough. Sunlight focused by the concave mirror on the tube heats the fluid—oil, in this case—to more than 500 degrees. The oil is then passed through heat exchangers to generate steam, the steam is used to drive turbines, and turbines drive generators.

In addition to these two solar-thermal facilities, Southern California Edison also receives electricity from a number of other renewable-energy projects. And the majority of this activity in renewable energy has occurred within the early 1980s. Clearly, the utility's policy shift has had a remarkable effect in stimulating the development of a diverse range of technologies. But perhaps we are seeing only the beginning, perhaps there are possible relationships among these different technologies that have yet to be perceived.

Many utility engineers remain skeptical of photovoltaics despite the experience of California utilities and the dozens of photovoltaic applications on large structures throughout the United States. While no one doubts the technical capabilities of the technology, skeptics see an inherent limitation in the facts that photovoltaics only work when the sun is shining and that efficiency is reduced by cloud cover. By contrast, a coal, oil, or nuclear facility can operate 24 hours a day regardless of weather.

The utility-scale plants built to date are all intended to address the utilities' need for "peak" power. If one looks at a load graph depicting when we use electricity and when we do not, it becomes immediately apparent that the average utility must generate sufficient power to cope with the peak load that hits in late afternoon and early evening. Annually, the peak load really "peaks" on the hottest summer days—air conditioners are on from midmorning to early evening. By two in the morning the load has fallen off considerably. The Sacramento Municipal Utility District's photovoltaic plant is specifically designed to address that utility's peak demands during summer days, precisely when the photovoltaics are generating the most electricity.

It is a curious fact that air conditioning is perhaps the single most absurdly wasteful use of energy. A well-designed home or commercial structure, possibly including some well-placed trees, can easily maintain cool temperatures on very hot days. Indeed, throughout much of the world's most arid regions whole villages are constructed to minimize solar gain, take advantage of prevailing winds, and remain cool on 100-degree-plus days. Advances in solar architecture in the United States over the past fifteen years have more than proven the feasibility of modifying an old structure or building a new home so that it remains cool on hot days. The house may not be frigid inside, as is possible with a typical air conditioning unit, but it will be considerably cooler than outside in direct sun. In any case, it is ironic that photovoltaics are being used in utility applications to meet the demand of air conditioning units that would not even be necessary if the buildings were designed correctly in the first place.

Clearly photovoltaic facilities can meet the technical requirements of utilities in generating sufficient electricity to cover peak loads. The price remains too high to be competitive without tax credits in most of the United States, but all indications are that the price will decline, regardless of tax-credit status. The only remaining issue is time on-line.

Theoretically, coal, nuclear, oil, natural-gas, and even wood-fired generating stations are capable of operating 24 hours a day, 365 days a year. In fact they never do. Coal and nuclear facilities may operate between 30 and 60 percent of their total life. The remainder of the time is spent in repairs, modifications, cleaning, and coping with occasional breakdowns. Regular maintenance work is planned for and the utility can easily purchase power from other utilities, or switch power over from another facility they operate, to make up the shortfall during the down periods. Break-downs can happen any time, and they can happen with little warn-ing. Within a few days, or a few hours, the entire generating plant may be shut down.

Lugo Station and other utility-scale photovoltaic plants are extremely reliable. So far, these new plants have generated maxi-mum output more than 92 percent of the theoretical maximum sun time. Every day, day after day, the photovoltaics consistently gen-erate a high percentage of their potential output. Obviously there are unknowns about the weather, particularly during the winter, but to some extent this can be offset by additional photovoltaic capac-ity to compensate for reduced efficiency in cloudy weather. The real problem appears to be storage—how to store energy for night and cloudy periods.

Heat can be stored for relatively short periods of time in var-ious liquids, including water and oil, and various solids such as salt. Electricity can be stored in batteries, or it can be used to per-form a chemical change in, for example, water, reducing it to con-stituent gases, which are then stored in tanks and later recombined as needed, giving off a portion of the electricity used to crack the water initially. Both techniques are well-established in research lit-erature if not in actual operations. Batteries are clearly workable on a small decentralized scale, in house and small commercial installations up to 10 kilowatts. Beyond that size the storage sys-

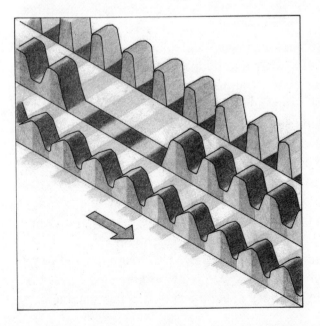

The use pattern of electricity over nine days. (a) How power is used: rising in the morning through the early evening and then dropping off. (b) The pattern of most conventional plants, showing a typ-ical shut-down for repairs for three days, or about 30 percent of the operating life-time of a given power plant. (c) A typical photovoltaic system. It generates full power in midday but no power at night. Based on cur-rent performance, utility-scale PV plants will perform for more than 90 percent of the system's working lifetime.

Use patterns of electrical energy and means of generation. At the bottom the four seasons are broken down, with winter on the left. Day and night are shown at bottom right.

Consumption pattern (a) reflects the demand for heating and lighting in the winter, the decline in spring, the peak demand in the summer when air conditioning is required (in most areas), and the drop back in fall. During the day, usage climbs until late afternoon and early evening and then begins to fall off until morning.

Conventional oil, gas, coal, and nuclear power plants can very precisely echo this pattern (b) but they may require repairs at any time, which result in interruptions of output.

Hydroelectric power, generally, is the most dependable, since (c) its output can remain steady for months on end. However, in years of little rain the output may be much lower, as indicated by the dotted line. Hydro facilities may also need to be shut down periodically.

Wind facilities (d) tend to be more unpredictable, with the highest output in winter, spring, and fall, and the lowest in summer. During the day cycle, wind generators tend to put out the most power during morning and afternoon periods when air masses are moving.

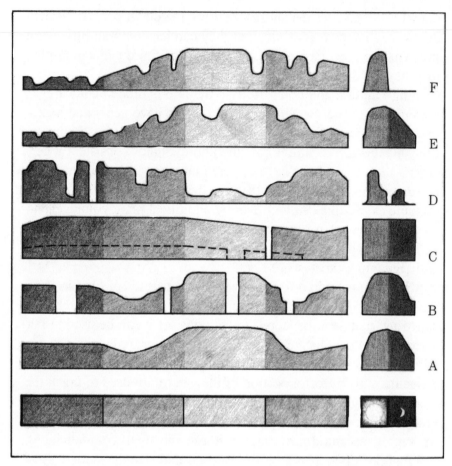

tems become somewhat less efficient as the capability of small batteries is stretched.

The most attractive options seem to be some form of heat storage and the cracking of water into hydrogen and oxygen. Heat storage might involve concentrating photovoltaics, similar to those United Energy Corporation now produces, and the pumping of hot water into underground storage tanks filled with salt. When the sun goes down, the heated salt would give off the energy stored during the day, keeping the hot water hot. Theoretically, the stored heat would be sufficient to power turbines, driving generators throughout the night. While such a system would not provide the same level of power output during the night as during the day, we do not need the same high level of output during the night.

The second possibility, cracking water into hydrogen and oxygen, has received considerable research attention over the past fifteen years. Hydrogen is a very clean-burning fuel that can be burned in conventional internal combustion engines. In an electro-chemical reaction, hydrogen and oxygen can be split apart within a batterylike device. Electricity charging two opposite poles, a cathode and an anode, can cause the water to split into hydrogen and oxygen, with one going to one pole and the other to the other pole. While the efficiency of this operation remains low, and the electrical energy required in proportion to the hydrogen produced thus high, this may be less an issue as photovoltaics come down in price.

Theoretically, a photovoltaic plant producing hydrogen would include a cracking facility, a fuel cell for recombining the two gases, and storage tanks to contain the gases. During the day a portion of the photovoltaic output would power the cracking unit. Hydrogen and oxygen would be drawn off and stored in tanks. At night the gases would be withdrawn and piped to the fuel cell. Within the fuel cell the recombination would occur, like a chemical fire, resulting in electricity and pure water. The water would be endlessly recycled—or the water source could be the ocean, and the photovoltaic plant could also function as a desalinization plant, producing pure water.

Another option that would allow storage of electrical power during night and cloudy periods would involve OTEGs, semiconductor products developed by Energy Conversion Devices. OTEGs convert heat directly into electricity. Concentrating and cogenerating photovoltaic modules producing heated water would be placed over an underground—earth-insulated—heat-storage chamber. Typically, the hot water would circulate in tubes within a tank of salt. During the day the salt would absorb the heat. At night, when the PV system was not generating electricity, the water would be recirculated through the bed of salt. The hot water would be piped through a screen, or sequence of screens, containing small OTEG semiconductors. Each OTEG would, like a single PV cell, put out a trickle of electricity converted from heat. The advantage of such a system would be its modularity. OTEGs, analogous to PV cells, are a highly modular technology that could be used on practically any scale.

Solar-thermal plants (e) tend to put out the most power in the summer and to have the least variation in output; this is why such plants can be very valuable in meeting peak summer-load demands. Photovoltaic (f) plants roughly parallel solar-thermal plants, which can have some storage capacity but do not generate any power during the night.

Distributors and Packagers

Throughout the United States there are a number of photovoltaic and renewable-energy companies that will assist customers in designing and purchasing a system. Some of these firms are purely regional distributors of photovoltaic products, others sell a broad line of small-scale power equipment, and a few operate mail order businesses. Like photovoltaic manufacturers, they represent fledgling organizations that perceive an enormous market but often feel caught between their own vision of a vast potential and the realities of "let's make a deal" down here on Earth. At the distributor level, the competition is as hot and wide open as on the manufacturer and research level. Distribution territories are not clearly defined, distribution agreements have not been fully worked out, if at all, and pricing stability does not exist. Further complicating the distributor's life is the 1984 entry of a low-cost Japanese product—the first of what may become a flood. But the distributors are still there, and they often represent an invaluable source of information about the regional problems of installing photovoltaic systems as well as their solutions.

Two California firms typify the work now being done by local distributors. Solarwest Electric (Santa Barbara) and Independent Power Company (Nevada City) both provide catalogs outlining a broad range of photovoltaic systems for water pumping, boats, recreational vehicles, small houses, medium-sized houses, and large homes. They also offer technical assistance in designing and installing a photovoltaic system.

Independent Power Company's catalog outlines eleven photovoltaic systems available with all necessary components in complete packages. The systems range from a single-module RV system at 110 watt-hours/day for $487, to a 1000 watt-hours/day medium-power system for a small house or cabin at $4000 on up to your "personal power company" package capable of providing practically all one's electrical needs in a large suburban home with more than 4000 watts output at a $20,000 price. If the market price of photovoltaics drops another 50 percent, as it did between 1980 and 1985, we may see a nearly 50 percent reduction in those prices by 1990. In any case, the packages are available, proven, and composed of highly durable components. And experienced assistance is available to guide a customer's search for the optimum system.

The mere existence of packaged systems reveals a degree of specialized knowledge about particular markets. We now know that most houses can be electrified with photovoltaic cells in systems that include 12 to 36 modules at about 40 watts output each, 12 to 40 batteries, one controller with meters, one inverter, and various lengths of wire for battery interconnects and module-to-controller wiring. We also know that in much of the United States in 1985 without tax credits the systems will cost, less installation labor, between $10,000 and $30,000.

Paralleling the development of photovoltaic distributors aimed at the consumer market are the growing marketing efforts of large engineering firms, which are beginning to sell their knowledge in the design of larger institutional and utility photovoltaic systems. Acurex Corporation was a major participant as a design firm in Sacramento Municipal Utility District's photovoltaic facility. From

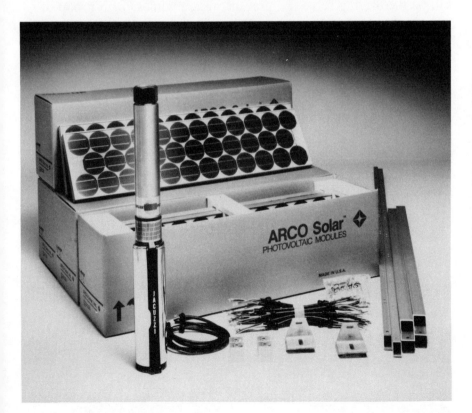

Characteristically, water pumping is often a remote-site power need not easily met by conventional energy sources. Windmills may be dependable but wind may not be, and gasoline or diesel pumps require constant attention. This whole system is marketed by Solarwest Electric. The cylindrical pump can be dropped into the well casing (carefully) and the accompanying modules can be installed on a stand-alone frame near the well. When the sun shines water pours forth.

(Source: Solarwest Electric)

there Acurex has begun to seek markets for similar facilities. In essence they have packaged the knowledge into a series of established design strategies that will yield a predictable result. In this way even the utility-scale facility can be marketed as a whole system, rather than as a logistics exercise customers must go through to assemble their own systems.

A new industry is like a new kid on the block: it tends to keep to itself and avoid contact with others until its relationship to the others is clearly visible. In the photovoltaic industry, we are witnessing the first results of a new industry's ties to related industries. The battery industry has now adapted both its product and its marketing approach to the needs of photovoltaic-system owners. Distributors have come into existence who are knowledgeable in the integration of the diverse components. It is probably inevitable that as the industry grows we will see as yet unimagined connections along with a host of new relationships among products, markets, other technologies, and industry organizations.

The technical connections will certainly yield some interesting products, but the personal ties behind those technical developments will be the driving force. At present we are witnessing a group of people who share a common vision just getting to know one another—the photovoltaic industry is that young.

SUNCELL

4: Crystal Tower

Amorphous Cells

A *morphous* means without definite order or precise structure—
in a word, chaotic. *Cell* means a narrow room used to con-
fine someone, a basic organizing element in Leninist politics, or
the smallest unit of biologically defined life. *Amorphous cells*
means chaos within order. The cells, in fact, are often small, rigid
squares of molecular chaos very precisely outlined by thin conductive lines of metal. Amorphous cells are analogous to the photovoltaic industry's current confusion and the chaos within the structure
of oil companies and the economy generally. Amorphous cells
made to date have anywhere from 30 to 60 percent the efficiency
of single-crystal or polycrystalline silicon cells per unit of area, but
they use a fraction of the material. Does this mean chaos is less
efficient than order while costing a lot less?

Amorphous photovoltaic cells are the industry's future. Single-
crystal and polycrystalline materials of every imaginable form and
shape will continue to be developed, manufactured, and used in a
variety of applications, but all indications are that various amorphous materials will surpass, by far, all other forms of photovoltaic
cell in terms of sheer volume produced.

In the early seventies, few people in the photovoltaic business
believed amorphous cells would really work except at the lowest
efficiencies and in the simplest applications—portable calculators,
for instance. By the mid-seventies, the work of Energy Conversion
Devices and RCA in amorphous materials was beginning to result
in cells that achieved reasonable efficiencies—more than 6 percent—and appeared to be mass producible. By the early eighties,
the basic parameters were known, manufacturing technology had
been developed, and amorphous materials were being made in
large quantities—primarily in Japan. The conventional wisdom in
physics had been that the semiconducting function of PVs was to
some extent reliant upon the materials' pure crystalline form. It
was—to some extent. Amorphous materials proved that the semiconducting event would still occur without a pure crystalline form.

In operation, amorphous silicon cells are practically identical to single-crystal cells. The barrier layer, or junction, occurs with a proper doping of impurities just as it does with single-crystal or polycrystal silicon. But the entire event happens inside a far smaller space, about a hundredth the thickness of a conventional single- or polycrystal cell. The sheer thinness of an amorphous cell is the reason why amorphous technology has received such attention. Amorphous cells are treated not as solid wafers but as thin coatings, more like paint than a solid object.

Theoretically, the advantage of amorphous cells was in their minimal use of material, but this meant that the thin coating had to be very precisely controlled, with no holes or breaks. Furthermore, the coating had to be made not only thin but with an extraordinary degree of precision and consistency, since even a slight variation in the quality of the coating would dramatically reduce efficiency. And if this were not enough, the coating had to receive a minute dose of impurities, typically boron and phosphorus, in extremely precise quantities. In measuring the production values of amorphous silicon cells, one uses measurements like atoms per cubic centimeter.

This centipede-like machine is the equivalent of a printing press, only it "prints" amorphous photovoltaic cells on a stainless steel sheet. Each segment is a vacuum chamber in which the various materials are deposited upon the stainless steel as it passes through. This machine is currently operated by Sovonics Solar Systems of Solon, Ohio.

(Source: Sovonics Solar Systems)

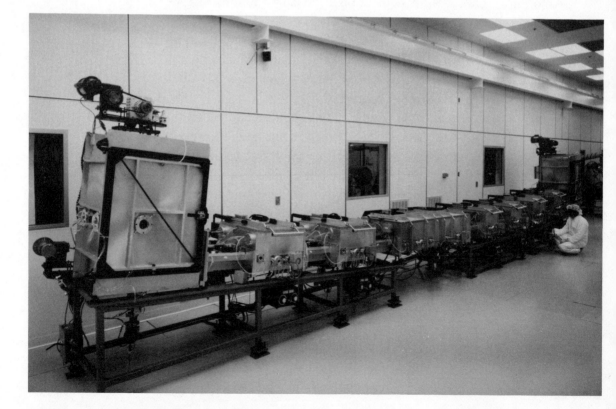

Researchers at Energy Conversion Devices and RCA were faced with a need not only to achieve the highest efficiency and lowest cost in the cell design, but also to practically invent the entire production process. Although some of the techniques were very similar to those used in semiconductor and integrated circuits, it remained to build an entire production machine and produce amorphous cells within the necessary tolerances. Both groups, particularly those at Energy Conversion Devices, built whole production lines, including new machines that could mass produce amorphous cells. ECD now has a separate division whose sole purpose is to build new production machinery for amorphous-cell production.

A machine that produces amorphous silicon cells was recently put into operation under a joint venture with ECD and Sharp Electronics of Japan. It looks like a cross between a printing press and a particle-beam accelerator. It is about five car lengths long, about 5 feet wide, and 15 feet high. It sits on a glass-smooth concrete floor in an antiseptic factory. This is a *clean* factory—there is no dust, no pile of junk in the corner, no gritty industrial look to it all.

A Sovonics Solar Systems's amorphous PV module. The entire module surface is covered by photovoltaic material. Most of the module's bulk is in framing, protective and backing materials surrounding the amorphous PVs and seals inside the frame to prevent intrusion of water. Only a fraction of the module's substance actually generates electricity.

(Source: Sovonics Solar Systems)

Even the employees tending the humming beast wear protective clothing to minimize the chance of errant dust particles ruining a production run. The machine is capable of producing about 3 megawatts of amorphous cells annually.

At one end of the machine small rolls of stainless steel sheet are mounted on guides. Like paper rolls on a newspaper printing press, the thin stainless is gradually fed into a sequence of production processes. The primary steps involve the deposition of silicon upon the stainless steel within vacuum chambers. Silicon, boron, and hydrogen in a gaseous state fill the vacuum chamber over the slowly moving stainless steel sheet. The gases are heated by radio frequency signals to a high temperature, which makes them glow. The ionized gas gradually settles on the stainless steel and bonds to its surface, which under a microscope would appear pitted and rough. After being coated with silicon, the material passes into another chamber, where the minute quantity of impurity is added to create the critical junction. Then the thin wires are added atop the coating, a matrix of metal lines that feel like printer's ink laid on another color. Finally, the entire sheet is coated with a glasslike material to protect it from weather and scratches. The final sheet is so thin it is flexible. The surface resembles the bluish black surface of a stagnant pond under an afternoon sky.

Early amorphous cells were vulnerable to weather and the degrading effects of long-term exposure to the sun. Now it appears that ECD, Solarex, Chronar, and ARCO Solar have solved these problems by developing more inherently stable amorphous materials and by adding coats over silicon, the semiconducting material. All indications suggest that amorphous cells in exterior applications will last at least fifteen years, with only a slight drop in efficiency over time. Single- and polycrystal cells will probably last more than twenty years, and Solar Energy Research Institute's goal for practically all photovoltaic products is twenty-five to thirty years.

Much of the current development work in amorphous cells is focused on the p-i-n-type cell. The p-i-n cell is composed of a sandwich of metal substrate—the foundation—a layer of hydrogenated silicon doped with phosphorus, an intrinsic layer of undoped hydrogenated silicon, a layer of hydrogenated silicon doped with boron, a layer of conductive metal oxide that allows electrons to travel out of the cell but is transparent so light passes through, and a layer of glass coating to protect the whole sandwich.

In 1976, the best amorphous-cell research was achieving 2 percent efficiency. In 1982, RCA's laboratories announced the development of a p-i-n-type amorphous cell capable of 10.1 percent efficiency. In 1984, Energy Conversion Devices announced the development of amorphous cells achieving 9.3 percent efficiency. ECD's short-term goal is 12 percent efficiency, and Stanford Ovshinsky, president and founder of ECD, insists that amorphous cells of 30 percent efficiency are possible. The RCA group is now a part of Solarex, operating as an amorphous division that will soon introduce new products.

Chronar Corporation is now producing p-i-n-type cells of a remarkably elegant design. Although they are only achieving 4 to 6 percent efficiency, the technology will clearly be improved sufficiently to increase average efficiency to more than 6 percent. Chronar, like Spire Corporation, is also focusing on the sale of turnkey photovoltaic factories designed to produce 1 megawatt annually. For about 7 million dollars, one can now purchase a Chronar factory and go into the business of making amorphous cells.

The price of amorphous, relative to its efficiency, is still too high to be widely competitive with utility-generated electricity in the United States. But like single-crystal and polycrystal silicon cells, amorphous is already competitive in many remote applications, in consumer products, and throughout much of the non-electrified world. And unlike single-crystal or polycrystal cells, amorphous cells present the possibility not only of low-cost photovoltaics but of very flexible and adaptable products. Amorphous cells effectively demonstrate that the generation of electrical current can occur in a space no thicker than 300 angstroms. What we had assumed could only occur in an electron-manufacturing facility the size of a city block can now occur in a film thinner than sprayed lacquer—spread over any roof that needs electricity.

An amorphous photovoltaic module now marketed by ARCO Solar. This starkly simple module, called a "Genesis G100," measures almost exactly one square foot and will generate 5 watts of power in full sunlight. In essence the module is little more than a piece of glass coated with amorphous materials surrounded by an injection molded plastic frame. The unit is designed for battery recharging, operating radios and other small appliances.

(Source: ARCO Solar)

The Renewed House: 1995

It looks like a relatively conventional split-level suburban home except the garage has been converted into a south-facing greenhouse filled with plants and small fruit trees. The roof tiles appear oddly shiny, as if there had been a recent rainfall, but the weather has been dry. The roof is composed almost entirely of glass tiles made by Chronar Corporation, while the garage carries high-efficiency polycrystalline panels made by Solarex.

Under the carport out in front of the garage-greenhouse is a small car with an extension cord extending from its front bumper to a plate in the wall of the house. Above the plate is a small door big enough for a dog to crawl through. Outside the small door is a metal rack with rails. A battery pack can be rolled out and into the car and the exhausted pack rolled back into the greenhouse for charging—the exchange takes about five minutes. But most of the time a trickle charge during the hiatus between dropping the kids off at school and going to the store in the afternoon is sufficient. The high-efficiency Solarex cells are specially designed to recharge car power packs.

As you walk up the front stairs, you pass a small outside light, barely noticeable, in the shrubbery. Atop its metal case is a shiny cross-hatched surface—amorphous cells. The light requires no external wiring; it's simply screwed into the wooden decking next to the walkway. At dusk it automatically comes on and a soft glow spreads across the otherwise dark walkway. As you walk up the path, the light's sensors detect the presence of a person and the light momentarily brightens as you pass. The kids on the block have devised a new form of hopscotch between the glowing lights on summer evenings.

The outside front door opens into a small vestibule where you leave your coat. The inside front door is so tight your ears detect the air pressure changes when it opens and closes. In the house it is very quiet. The thick insulation in the walls and double-paned windows keep the exterior noises outside. The house is warm—heat is evenly distributed in air that appears to be gently moving. It

A fully solar home with greenhouse and hot-water collectors integrated into one package. The home's woodstove is located beneath the hot-water collectors, allowing water to be circulated around the flue for additional heating on coldest days. The PV panels cover much of the roof (dark) and are composed of amorphous-coated glass. Nonelectric glass panels cover areas between the PV panels (light). Typically, such glass panels could be coated with heat-reflective coating on the inside and heat-sensitive materials on the surface. On cold days the glass would turn translucent and let sunlight into the plenum space within the roof (see detail), warming the air circulating within. The light would pass through holes drilled in plywood subroofing, or some other open matrix. As the temperature rose, the coating on the glass would turn cloudy and block the sunlight. Such thin coatings, sensitive to light and temperature, are already available.

circulates slowly through plenum spaces in the floor and ceiling. The house is rarely cooler than 60 degrees F, even when the outside temperature is 35 degrees F, but on those really cold nights the high-efficiency fireplace is stoked up with wood. The air chambers surrounding the fire allow heated air to be drawn from outside and funneled into the ceiling plenum spaces.

The kitchen has its back to the fireplace wall. Dishwasher, refrigerator, oven, and stove all vent their excess heat into the plenum space. On hot days the same air-circulation system allows the warm air to be circulated out of the house, with the aid of a heat pump that works off the difference between the home's interior temperature and the temperature of dirt under the greenhouse. The refrigerator-freezer and all other appliances use the most advanced mechanical devices, motors, and control circuitry. They are lighter, simpler, and far more efficient than contemporary appliances.

Light switches in every room sense the presence of people and turn on, or off, unless they are overriden by a manual switch. The incandescent lightbulbs commonly last four to six years and use about 70 percent less energy than contemporary bulbs. The overall energy consumption for lighting is less than a third of contemporary consumption, yet there is no noticeable difference in lighting levels.

On a wall near the greenhouse door is a small panel with a few gauges and a slowly moving piece of graph paper behind a small window. Above it are electronic barometer and thermometer readouts. This device is a small computer connected to sensors throughout the house. It is capable of tracking all interior and exterior weather conditions for a year. It adjusts the various vents controlling air flow into and out of the plenum spaces and monitors the home's photovoltaic output and electrical consumption. It is also capable of reading voice commands, but no one likes to talk to it, though occasionally someone will yell, "It's too hot."

The large expanse of double-paned glass facing the home's southern side is coated with a thin film that allows solar heat to enter the house but not to leave by reflection. In the summer, enough reflected sunlight can enter the house through the large south-facing windows to heat the living room. Thin Venetian blinds are lowered on the hotter days. Each blind is coated with amorphous silicon. The additional power generated by the blinds is

A typical row house with hot-water panels on the rear of the building and two skylights placed across the roof and angled towards the sun. Atop the north-facing skylights are south-facing PV panels. The front awnings of the house also contain small PV panels. In New York City, Baltimore, Philadelphia, Boston, Seattle, and San Francisco there are hundreds of thousands of two- to four-unit buildings of this row-house variety. These buildings have been or can be retrofitted with insulation, double-pane windows, and full solar water heating. Depending on a building's location, orientation, and local climate, it can be heated by direct solar gain, with the assistance of a small wood stove, or by roof-mounted hot-water collectors circulating hot water through floors.

a modest addition but it helps cope with high demands for electricity in the summer—particularly for car trips.

In the living room, hung like a huge painting, is a 4- by 6-foot flat-plate television screen. It uses less than a quarter of the energy a contemporary tube-type television consumes and produces brighter images with higher resolution in 3-D format. Watching this television is like looking out a window.

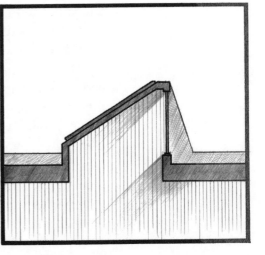

In the kitchen is a small flashlight with a surface composed of amorphous silicon in a diamond pattern. It lies on the table next to a picture-book-size television, also coated in amorphous silicon. The two objects are sitting in a triangle of afternoon sun. Everyone in the house knows that if those two things are left in that place on the table every day, or almost every day, they will remain charged.

In the bathroom, hot water is supplied by small roof-mounted panels integrated with garage-roof photovoltaics. Small electric "demand" heaters are located in the kitchen and bathroom faucets to boost the temperature if necessary.

The entire house is 100 percent solar. With the exception of a small quantity of firewood, the house receives no outside energy or fuel. All the technology required to modify an existing home in this way is either on the market now, in research projects now underway, or likely to be available within five to ten years. The completed home would require sewage, water, and telephone hook-ups. However, current developments in a wide range of areas suggest the possibility of recycling water systems with rainwater replenishment, allowing waste materials to be turned into fertilizer. They would eliminate the entire water and sewage hookup. And developments in cellular radio telephone service suggest that whole neighborhoods might need only one telephone-receiving line tied into a single cellular receiving unit. All telephones in that neighborhood would call into or receive calls from the central unit. The telephone, including the small computer that kept track of the household's friends, acquaintances, and business associates, would be powered by an amorphous panel the size of a matchbook cover and you could make calls from anywhere, including your car.

Such a totally self-contained house, cluster of houses, or apartment building is now possible, and building such structures might be the most efficient means of transforming energy towards our ends. Some might consider this building the ultimate American dream—a self-contained structure allowing totally mobile and rootless living with no connection to the community at large. Paradoxically, a totally solar home would demand of us a greater perception of our environment locally, regionally, and on the scale of the universe. Those who live in solar houses often mention that their homes seem to breathe on their own, and that they feel more in touch than ever with the elements—as if their houses were extensions of their senses.

Solar Wheels

Since the beginning of the automobile age, we have been expanding the road network in peristaltic waves of concrete and asphalt construction. Few politicians have said no to roads and survived the next election. Expanding roads has been an American activity for more than seventy years.

In 1985 the traffic in practically every major American city is worse than ever. Interstate highways and local feeder roads are often at or over capacity. It is as if a steady stream of liquid were being poured into a wine bottle—as the liquid reaches the narrow neck it accelerates. We are now nearing the neck of the bottle. The number of new cars on the road in many cities has been increasing steadily for years. Within five to eight years, the problem will reach crisis proportions, with traffic jams and even gridlocks of epic proportions. With few exceptions, most highways cannot be expanded due to very high costs. And since much of the highway and local road system is now in need of extensive reconstruction, it is doubtful that we will be able to afford any serious expansion programs.

Extensive traffic congestion will exacerbate air pollution as thousands of idling engines in stop-and-go traffic cough up pollutants. In the late sixties, when the lead was still in gasoline and most of us got eight to ten miles per gallon, we began to realize just how serious the pollution was. Then our cars were equipped with antipollution equipment and we began buying a lot more small cars. These measures helped for a time, but now the combination of more cars, denser traffic, growing congestion, and the sheer volume of pollutants that enters the atmosphere anyway is resulting in a growing pollution problem over many cities—Los Angeles, Denver, Dallas, Houston, San Jose, San Francisco, Tokyo, São Paulo, Mexico City, and countless others. The pollution problems we are soon to face in the United States will no doubt result in a second wave of interest in nonpolluting automobiles.

In the late sixties and through much of the seventies there has

A solar car conceived as a small (for four to six person) vehicle with an exterior skin covered in amorphous photovoltaic material. It would continually recharge its battery pack in the sun and require only occasional recharging from the home system. The car could have a range of 125–200 miles. Specially designed hub motors in each wheel would allow maximum traction and control—infinitely variable four-wheel drive. At bottom are the three basic methods of powering a car. (a) An internal combustion engine with rear-mounted tank. The fuel could be gasoline, hydrogen, or ethanol. (b) A hydrogen tank supplying gas to the fuel cell at the back of the vehicle. Hydrogen burns chemically in the fuel cell, giving off electricity, which is wired to a motor controller and two electric motors driving the front wheels. (c) A simple battery, controller, and single-motor drive system.

been considerable activity in electric-car development. Numerous prototypes and a few working production-line vehicles have resulted but, perhaps more importantly, the feasibility of electric cars has been clearly proven. While many prototypes were limited

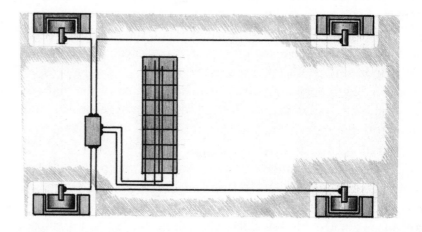

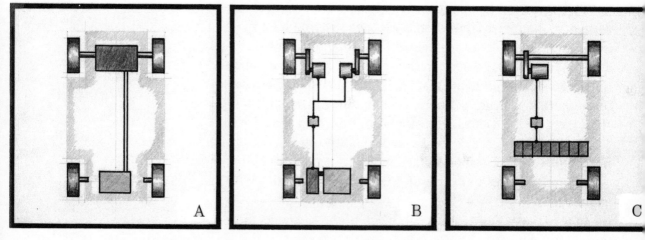

A

B

C

to short range—between 60 and 90 miles—on a full charge, research efforts indicate that an electric car with a range of 150 miles plus is quite feasible. But of course the establishment of electric-car technology involves a substantial, multibillion dollar outlay in new tooling and manufacturing techniques. Why would auto companies spend that kind of money?

The existing internal-combustion-engine-powered automobile represents an extraordinarily high level of technology. The car has received perhaps more research and development attention—and more money—than any other invention known to humankind. But the engine, and the car in some circumstances, has reached certain limitations. Certainly the internal combustion engine can be improved still more; new technologies already in design stages will result in higher efficiencies and more miles to the gallon. Hydrogen could be used as a fuel, eliminating the pollution problems inherent in burning hydrocarbon fuels—gasoline and diesel fuel. And to some extent hydrogen may become a viable fuel, allowing internal combustion engines to remain in use. But other forces may result in the development of electric cars.

An internal combustion engine involves reciprocating pistons that turn a crankshaft—a transfer of reciprocating motion to rotary motion that results in a degree of lost energy no matter how efficient the components might be. By comparison, an electric motor is a rotary machine; it has no reciprocating parts. Furthermore, an electric motor is only one moving part within a stationary case, not hundreds of moving parts that all must work in perfect unison. Per unit of horsepower, electric motors can be lighter, more efficient, longer-lasting, and much cleaner, quieter and simpler to maintain than diesel or gasoline engines. Since an electric motor develops nearly its full power potential at a standing start, only a simple transmission is needed to transfer power from the motor to the wheels.

We are already seeing a trend in favor of small citycars, three- and four-cylinder cars designed almost entirely for city driving or short commute trips. The widespread use of citycars reflects a gradual change in the way cars are used, a tendency to use cars for local trips rather than long-distance trips. The combination of citycar use and development, air-pollution problems, inherent simplicity, and potentially lower production costs forms a context for electric-car development on a substantial scale. Adding to the likelihood of this course: in the mid-1990s world oil production will probably peak and then steadily decline in production levels. This will result in steady increases in fuel costs, driven up by shrinking supplies, and the likely need to finance road reconstruction work with gas taxes.

The technological options lie in two primary areas—battery and fuel-cell technology. Batteries are clearly workable now but they are heavy and require replacement after two to four years of use. New battery technology suggests that there are methods of reducing weight and increasing a car's range without sacrificing battery life, but it remains to be seen whether this technology can be translated to practical production-scale devices. Fuel cells are receiving growing attention as a means of generating electricity from a fuel—almost any fuel. Fuel cells are somewhat similar to batteries in operation, only they do not store energy. Instead, fuel is metered into the cell, where it "burns" in an electrochemical "fire" giving off electricity in the process. Typically, fuel cells could be used in an electric car, and have been used in small test vehicles, to "burn" hydrogen stored in a tank and provide electricity for the car's motor.

Beryl and Jim Plantz are among thousands of "Snowbirds"—retirees who live in RVs on the road—who migrate south for the winter. They travel and live in a converted intercity bus electrified by ARCO PV modules. The modules recharge a 12 volt dc battery that powers lights, television, CB radio and a water pump.

(Source: ARCO Solar)

Hydrogen is a major unknown. Various research efforts have clearly proven the feasibility of burning hydrogen in an engine, and in a fuel cell, but those within the energy industry who have studied it remain divided about its potential. On the one hand hydrogen is a very clean and high-powered fuel that could be produced in sufficient quantities for vehicle fuel. Hydrogen is produced now for a variety of industrial applications and has been produced for many decades. On the other hand, hydrogen production, typically by cracking water, requires a substantial quantity of energy itself and is not very efficient. Hydrogen is also very volatile: once ignited it burns explosively.

The efficiency of hydrogen production is often measured in relation to the quantity of fossil fuels consumed to crack hydrogen from water. On that basis, hydrogen production is almost analogous to nuclear power—one burns up a huge amount of existing energy in its construction that may or may not return an energy "profit" within its useful lifetime. With solar energy, either a solar-thermal or photovoltaic power plant, the economics may be quite different, since the solar source is effectively inexhaustible and the technology will probably last longer than any comparable fossil or nuclear facility. The potential of hydrogen as a fuel probably rests entirely on whether its production with solar sources is economically sound and whether a safe means of storing hydrogen can be found.

Photovoltaic-powered vehicles already exist in the form of golf carts that recharge themselves "on the green" and a few personal cars whose owners have built their own photovoltaic systems. The physical area of a car roof is not sufficient to generate enough electricity to fully power a car, but if the home or garage includes a charging panel, then the car can be plugged in when not in use or a second battery pack can be charged while one is driving. In use, electric cars are extremely smooth and quiet. One has a "gas" pedal, a brake, and a forward and reverse shift. The car will accelerate very smoothly from a dead stop to 60 miles per hour, and the tires will make more noise than the motor.

Given research in amorphous cells to date, it appears quite possible that within ten years we might see an electric car that is effectively "painted" with amorphous material. With most of the vehicle's exterior skin covered with photovoltaics, the car's battery pack would be recharged almost constantly. While a second battery pack would probably still be necessary, it might not be used very often considering how much time cars sit in parking lots. Curiously, the automobiles now being produced are very boxy and have few compound curves; thus it would be relatively simple to cover these flat surfaces with an amorphous skin.

Although advances in battery technology may allow larger and heavier vehicles to be powered with batteries, it is doubtful that this will occur. The concentrated weight of a bus, truck, or train is so great that a battery pack of sufficient size, giving enough range, would be substantial. This is where hydrogen may become viable—as a fuel for large and heavy vehicles. Generally, the turnover of heavy vehicles is far slower than with cars; the former last longer and there is a tendency to optimize their maintenance to achieve the maximum vehicle life. The investment necessary to modify a conventional heavy vehicle to burn hydrogen would not be a major investment relative to the total cost of a typical new truck, bus, or locomotive. Furthermore, these vehicles tend to operate on known routes over and over again rather than freely throughout the transportation networks. This eliminates the distribution problems associated with using hydrogen in automobiles.

We may see the development of small electric cars designed to be recharged by photovoltaics both on the car and on one's home. This is likely to occur in the mid-1990s. Use of hydrogen as a fuel may occur on heavy vehicles in the 1990s but would probably not become widespread until well into the next century. More than any other renewable technology, photovoltaics present the possibility of widespread development of electric cars, and possibly of hydrogen, due primarily to the high likelihood that PVs will become substantially cheaper than conventional electric sources in the nineties.

Oddly, the development of electric cars may represent a major market entry point for photovoltaics. We tend to be very conservative in our attitudes about home, but nearly frivolous when it comes to automobiles. We are more likely to try something new on the car than on the house. Plus, we spend more on automobile energy than on electrical energy. In much of the United States, and the world, oil and therefore gasoline prices are considerably higher than electrical prices per unit of energy. So, we may see photovoltaics on garages before we see them on houses.

Electric Towers

High-rise buildings are paper factories that gobble electrical energy at a prodigious rate. Typically, they are overlit with glaring panels of fluorescent lights day and night. They are overheated in the winter and overcooled in the summer. The air conditioning systems in many highrises are required as much to cool the buildings in summer as to exhaust the heat produced by the excessive lighting all year round. The whole idea of a climate-controlled building is both the result of decades of cheap energy and a statement of just how out of touch many of us are with the forces of nature that affect our lives.

We've built the power plants and transportation systems to feed the high-rise buildings that form the structure of downtown business districts while simultaneously sealing ourselves within those buildings to avoid the air pollution, wind, and noise that we've created in building them. Ostensibly, the buildings are constructed to perform logical, necessary, and ultimately profitable business functions. Yet they are as much a response to the demands of business as to the chaos around them. Do we, in the process of creating order, necessarily create more disorder?

High-rise buildings are unlikely simply to go away; nor are they likely to become the world's largest ghost towns, as intriguing as that idea might be. What will we do with them?

A few blocks from California's state capitol building in Sacramento sits a block-square office building known as the Bateson Building. It was built under the administration of Governor Jerry Brown in the late seventies and early eighties as a demonstration of solar energy and conservation technology. The building receives a major portion of its heating and air conditioning energy from the sun and involves a wide range of subtle architectural approaches aimed at decreasing energy consumption. Typically, lighting is oriented to specific tasks: small and movable lighting units are located near desks and office machines where the light is needed. The Bateson Building could be a harbinger of things to come, as are the dozens of similarly designed all or partially solar-heated buildings throughout the United States.

Energizing a conventional highrise with solar heat and photovoltaic electricity is usually not feasible unless its occupants make some basic changes in their temperature and lighting demands—which now could be called luxurious. If the energy demand were to decline, and if projected efficiency increases in photovoltaic technology prove to be accurate, then we might see the development of high-rise buildings that are totally, or almost totally, self-contained.

The exterior skin of a typical high-rise building can be concrete, steel, aluminum, marble, glass, or brick. Generally the skin

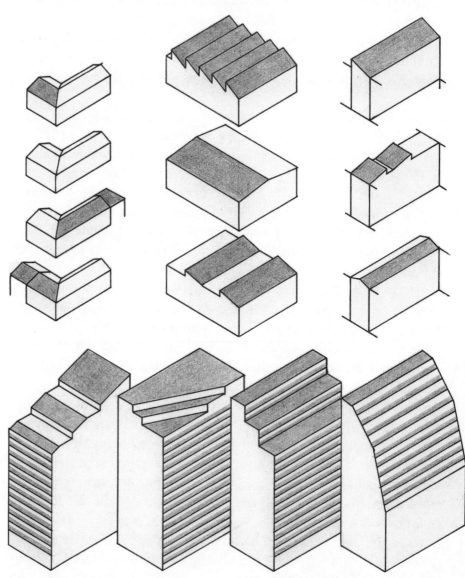

Integrating photovoltaics into the roofs and walls of buildings. Generally, we will probably see the development of inexpensive amorphous materials for use on home and small commercial buildings, with more expensive amorphous cascade cells, polycrystalline, and crystalline cells designed for large commercial structures.

is just that; it has little or no structural value relative to the entire building's structural frame. In most high-rise buildings, the exterior walls are composed of more than 40 percent glass; in some, practically the entire wall is glass, interrupted only by joining metal frames.

Highrises are often high; thus they present a huge area to the sun. While this facade may be in shadow part of the day due to surrounding highrises, the vast proportion of new structures, at least in U.S. cities, are no longer built out to the property line, as once was the case. Instead, they are often set in a plaza or back from the street. As a result, there tends to be more open-air space between buildings, and therefore more sunlight penetrating the canyons between them. The roofs of most highrises, and often the top floors as well, are almost always in total sunlight all day and all year long.

High-rise buildings, like it or not, are also very good solar collectors. Of the sun they receive through sealed windows, a considerable quantity is captured in the building's floors, walls, furniture, and air. Late on summer afternoons, most high-rise buildings become very warm on the western side, a problem that often causes the air conditioning system to work overtime.

There will come a point in the commercialization of amorphous silicon cells when it will be possible to integrate them with wall-panel materials for high-rise buildings. If half a high-rise wall were covered in amorphous cells and the other half in glass—transparent—there is no doubt that the building could receive a substantial amount of energy from its own walls. Even those walls in shadow would produce some energy. The floor area within 5 feet of all windows could be covered in glass tile coated with amorphous cells. The tile would absorb heat, generate electricity, and give off the heat later as the building cooled down in the evening.

Atop the roof there might be concentrator cells cooled by water. High-efficiency concentrators would provide additional electricity while also providing hot water for building heating and kitchen service. Additional concentrating units might be located on the higher floors facing south. Even windowshades could include amorphous cells to further increase the electrical output. Many of the building's office machines might also be powered by small amorphous panels located on the machines, reducing electrical demands upon the building and the need for cords to outlets.

It is conceivable that such a building might not even need a heating or air conditioning system, at least not a large centralized unit. If the building were properly designed, and if occupants did not require the maintenance of exactly 70 degrees no matter what was going on outside, such a building might be, intrinsically, a huge heating and cooling unit.

One exterior deck on the angled, south-facing side of a typical hotel or apartment building. At lower right is a cross-section. The panels below the railing are polycrystalline PVs, the sun-shading louvers are aluminum coated with amorphous PVs, and the tiles, both on the deck floor and the building's side wall, are glass PV tiles—amorphous. The louvers keep sun off the deck on hot summer days while generating electricity. They also include hot-water piping. The floor and wall tiles generate electricity, and warm water circulates through the room's floor for space heating. A small set of batteries would be contained beneath the railing in the triangular space. All wiring and hot-water piping would be totally confined to each room; thus the room would only have to be connected to the central hotel/apartment building water source and phone lines, not to hot-water pipes or electric wires. Most of the technology required to do this is now available.

Sun Economy

There is no single product now on the market with the broad applicability of photovoltaic cells. Nor is there any other product on the market likely to change not only how we generate electricity but how we think about energy.

Photovoltaics are like the main course in a dinner of renewable energy sources. Without PVs the meal would be meager indeed, but with PVs it could be a feast. Photovoltaics complete the spectrum of renewable technologies and make it possible practically to eliminate all fossil and nuclear energy use within a matter of decades. Eliminating fossil and nuclear fuels means not only eliminating the economics of large-scale centralized power plants but also a steady decrease and eventual end to the pollution caused by fossil- and nuclear-fuel use. Further, the decline in fossil-fuel dependency in the United States will inevitably result in reductions in military activity, since the need to protect sources of imported oil will diminish. Domestically the development of photovoltaics, and a wide range of renewable technologies, need not be an exercise in technological centralization and further specialization, but rather a transition to decentralized, accessible, and inherently more democratic means of utilizing the energy income we already receive.

When major oil discoveries were made in the early years of this century, the most optimistic progressives made bold pronouncements about how oil would revolutionize our world. Many of the same people made similar statements about automobiles and airplanes. And they were right. Within twenty years, which is a very short time, the Model T evolved from a neighborhood curiosity into a national phenomenon—13 *million* Model Ts were produced. As a society, the United States went from no oil and no cars to plenty of oil and millions of cars in a historical period of only two decades.

What observers saw in oil, in contrast to wood and coal, was a fluid with a high-energy density that could be pumped, moved, stored, and used in a variety of ways. They saw intrinsic advantages in this new stuff—elemental differences between it and what had been used up to that point. Similarly, they saw the automobile as a breakthrough not just in personal transport but in how the need of transportation was fulfilled and in the social implications of how it was done. Although oil and car prices were a major factor in the development of the new technologies, it was the intrinsic advantages that truly "sold" these products. The same seems true of photovoltaics—the technology could not only develop very rapidly but a sequence of social changes could parallel its development. Just as the car and airplane required a liquid fuel that just happened to be discovered at the right moment so also does the PV industry require a new view of energy, a view that is now rapidly evolving in the utility industry and society at large. The most critical marketing program for the development of all renewables, and particularly photovoltaics, was played out in the media between 1973 and 1979. The "energy crisis" provided the impetus we needed to begin changing our understanding of energy.

The development of the oil industry, and of automobiles and airplanes, shows us that wholly new industries can grow very rapidly *if* the intrinsic advantages of the technology are so great that they solve many problems at once, are widely accessible, and are aligned with a wide variety of already established social and economic trends. Clearly, PVs fit the bill. They are the kind of development that revolutionizes technology and causes the creation of wholly new industries and institutions.

A measure of how a technology is and will be accepted is who adopts the technology first and why. When the most conservative industries in the society adopt a technology first, despite its high price and somewhat foreign qualities, one can be sure that big changes are in the air. As already noted, utilities are steadily becoming more involved in photovoltaics. Oil companies that have paid relatively little attention to other developments in renewable energy are heavily committed to photovoltaics. Railroads, perhaps the most conservative and financially tight industry in the United States, are also heavily invested in photovoltaics, with more than 350 installations. City, county, and regional governments, as well as some states—notably Massachusetts and California—are committed to PVs both in policy and practicality, as shown in specific government-financed projects. In all these businesses and institutions, *any* technology is viewed with great suspicion until its value has been proven beyond a doubt. Local government, utilities, and oil companies rarely make frivolous purchases of new tools.

Why have three major California utilities become involved in PVs? Why has a major southern utility, Alabama Power, entered into an agreement with Chronar Corporation to make and distribute PVs? Obviously, these utilities see the technology, to some extent, as a major force in their future. But why have they made such uncharacteristic moves?

Critics of the utility industry have often stated that the industry's primary problem is the lack of competition. Since utilities exist within regulated domains, observers have claimed, they need not be concerned with outsiders upsetting the comfortable process of selling electricity. To a great extent that *was* true when energy prices were more stable and oil, coal, and nuclear prices were about the same, but these conditions have changed. Now we have a situation in which one utility in the Northeast charges more than 17 cents a kilowatt hour while in the West others charge less than a third of that price. And when a few nuclear power plants come on-line in the late eighties, some utilities may be forced to sell electricity at even higher prices—more than 20 cents per kilowatt hour. A utility may not be able to pick up its power plants and move on to the next region when the economy is no longer favorable, but customers can—and they do. Sudden rises in electrical prices to commercial customers have caused an exodus of industry out of certain areas. Increasingly, U.S. utilities will soon be competing with one another, and their regions will be competing for industry.

Adding to the competitive regional pressures are new sources of competition—independent producers and probably photovoltaics. Independents can include everything from a large commercial farmer going into on-site power production to a major corporation building a cogeneration plant and cutting the utility line, or at least reducing utility-power purchases. In some areas of the United States, the disparity between utility prices at 10 cents per kilowatt hour or greater and independent power production costs at 4 to 8 cents per kilowatt hour may increase due to new power plants coming on-line. Meanwhile, photovoltaics, particularly amorphous PVs, will decline in price. Inevitably, it will become cheaper to install PVs on your home, office, or industrial roof than to buy utility power. PV technology does not simply mean that utilities must compete with a new form of electrical generation; it means competition with a form that does not necessarily require utility involvement through connection to the grid.

In the mid-seventies, Detroit auto makers were in serious financial difficulty, but they rebounded and are now making an increasingly competitive product. Indeed, Ford Motor Company, perhaps more than any other auto corporation, not only rebounded financially but made some dramatic and courageous marketing moves toward using highly sophisticated designs that go against the historical grain of automobile styling and marketing. Utilities are in a similar bind. They are faced with a wholly new technology that not only rewrites the book of electrical generation but is being aggressively marketed by, no less, the Japanese, Europeans, and American oil companies.

Utilities are faced with a situation analogous to that of the railroads in the period between 1910 and 1930. Like utilities, they provided a service, passenger trains, that was regionally regulated and not subject to direct consumer control; consumers could not buy a train and drive it when they felt like it. But suddenly the railroads were faced not just with automobiles but with a transition from transportation as a corporate service to transportation as a consumer product. Utilities must cope with photovoltaics not just as a new generating technology but as a structural change in the way energy is marketed and used. The *means* of electrical generation is now a consumer product.

Already there are many indications, aside from obvious instances like Lugo Station and the Sacramento Municipal Utility District's plant, that the utility industry is meeting the challenge. The three most notable trends are the rapid growth in small-scale

Photovoltaic Industry Potential, 1990–2030

Year:	1990	2000	2010	2020	2030
Output	40	4707	66,825	928,527	13,467,726
Homes	41,500	588,375	8,353,125	118,565,000	1,683,250,000
Price	$2.40	$ .50	$ .40	$ .30	$ .30
Income	$796 million	$2,353 billion	$26,730 billion	$474,263 billion	$4,040,317 trillion
Jobs in industry	1,600	188,280	1,670,625	23,213,175	336,675,000

Output: Megawatts per year output
Homes: 50 percent of annual production, 4 kw/4000 watts average per house
Price: Average price all types of PV modules, amorphous dominates from 1990s on
Income: Gross income annually to entire industry
Jobs: 40 jobs per Mw in 1990, 30 in 2000, 25 in 2010 and after due to automation

power generation, fossil fueled or renewable; the decline of nuclear power; and the acceptance of conservation as a legitimate strategy.

How these trends will play out is as yet anyone's guess, but perhaps Alabama Power's recent move toward producing and distributing photovoltaics is a harbinger of things to come. This one step, whether it results in any serious action or not, represents a major shift in utility policy—from selling electricity alone to selling the means of generation and, potentially, developing a whole network of independent power producers.

By returning to the example of Southern California Edison, we can construct a hypothetical scenario outlining how the utility industry could change over the next 25 to 50 years.

SCE is now unusually dependent upon oil and natural gas to fuel its steam-generating stations—expensive sources compared to coal and hydroelectric. Hydro sources have, for the most part, been extensively developed, and coal is out of the question in Southern California due to air pollution. Clearly SCE, more than most utilities, is in need of a wholly new strategy. And it has already begun developing such a strategy.

SCE could become a distributor, installer, and financier of photovoltaic systems for residential and commercial use. Given the utility's considerable purchasing power, a few substantial orders for PV systems would, by virtue of scale, result in a decline in price. The cost of the PVs to customers would simply be treated as a monthly expense—the electric bill would remain the same or decline. SCE could market fully independent systems, with batteries, to rural customers who now rely on a long, thin thread of utility wire that is costly to maintain and subject to breakage. Possibly within ten to twenty years, whole rural regions would no longer require utility lines, which would mean a dramatic cost reduction for SCE. And rural electricity would probably cost less, not more. New developments in outlying areas could be totally solar, requiring no power lines and relying on SCE only for system installation and occasional maintenance.

Throughout the Los Angeles basin, SCE could sell and install residential PV systems connected to the grid. Inevitably, these home systems would generate a surplus of electricity during midday. To some extent, this peaking of output would coincide with the peak demands of commercial users. As suburban PV systems became more common, they would generate sufficient electricity for midday commercial users. Homeowners would travel to work, and the electricity their home would be generating in their absence would go with them.

While marketing PV systems, SCE could also market insulation and solarization programs. In one fell swoop, a single home would be transformed into a nearly 100 percent solar home. Ironically, the development of photovoltaics as roof materials, at a lowered cost, might even allow the house to remain all-electric, replete with solar-photovoltaic-powered electric stove, oven, and heating system. The marketing of the solar energy "package" could be just that—a package. Many customers do not care about kilowatts and megawatts; all they want to know is Where do I stick the plug? and How much is the bill? SCE, working with local contractors, could develop a solarization package that would result in a simple transaction translated to a monthly bill.

On the coastal bluffs overlooking the Pacific, on the mountains above the movie star "cottages" at Malibu Beach, and atop thousands of buildings in windy locations, SCE and possibly third-party financing partners could install all scales of wind generators. Linked together into a single regional system, or into a series of more local systems, a network of wind turbines might meet a substantial portion of the city's night and cloudy-period electrical demand. In the ocean off Los Angeles are offshore oil-drilling rigs. When those wells run dry, or when demand is insufficient to justify their continued use, the platforms might be converted to thermal-gradient generators. A cluster of vertical generators would float around the platform and perhaps a forest of wind turbines would stand where the drilling tower once stood. Technically, this is possible in 1985, and the price is either close to competitive or soon will be.

SCE, like most utilities, is continually faced with the need to accommodate major industrial customers and their often enormous demands for electricity. Turning on a factory is analogous to plugging in every single appliance in your house and turning them all on simultaneously. Needless to say, most commercial users typically require a team of utility engineers to assess their needs and assist in the design of the facility's electrical system. It does not take any great stretch of the imagination to envision the relatively minor shift required. The same utility engineers could assist a major commercial customer in designing a building or modifying an existing one so that it required much less heating energy and could be fully heated and electrified by the sun. In most cases this process would result in the installation of high-efficiency cogenerating photovoltaic modules that would provide both electricity and hot water.

If one proposed to the oil industry that it aggressively develop the technology for photovoltaic-powered automobiles, one would probably receive a polite no thanks. The industry, as an industry, would probably perceive such a move as threatening its continued sale of oil in the short term. But what if one went to only one oil company? And what if one was aligned with a major utility and an auto maker? What if SCE, Ford, and ARCO Solar—a typical consortium—entered into a quiet agreement to produce and market PV-powered citycars? And what if the first primary market was Los Angeles and similarly hazy Sunbelt cities?

The auto maker in such a deal would no doubt see it as a way to get a major jump on the competition. The oil company would also see it as a competitive move in a direction other oil companies are not likely to take lightly. The utility would see it as a means of expanding the marketability of photovoltaics and of entering into the business of providing energy for transportation. And the city government, as well as many residents, might see it as a move toward improving the quality of the environment and thus improving property values in an urban region that, owing to its horrible air, is now losing population and value as an attraction.

Encouraging the rapid development of electric cars for short-haul commuting and shopping would be a major breakthrough in improving environmental quality. By the mid 1990s, electric cars might also be feasible at a lower price than conventional internal combustion cars. Maintenance costs would be lower; that's practically a certainty. Production costs theoretically could be lower. And "fuel" costs would probably be lower. Moreover, electric cars would not only reduce air pollution but practically eliminate the engine-noise pollution now taken for granted.

In addition to assisting in the development and marketing of electric cars, SCE could also develop large-scale solar-thermal- or photovoltaic-powered hydrogen-generation facilities. Hydrogen and possibly ethanol would be used as basic fuels for trucks, buses, long-distance cars, and locomotives. They might also be used as fuels for aircraft and ships.

Current planning in Los Angeles and San Diego and in the cities of Orange County includes the development of light-rail, or trolley, projects. SCE could develop photovoltaic facilities to provide power for these systems, allowing the development of transportation systems not dependent upon the integrity of the utility grid or on oil availability.

Considering that SCE is now generating more power from solar-thermal and photovoltaic facilities than any other utility, and that this development has occurred within about six years, it is conceivable that a nearly total conversion to renewables is feasible within two to four decades. As a crash program, conversion might be possible within 25 years. In any case, the potential exists and is based on technology that is now available.

The result? A pollution-free Los Angeles owing to the widespread use of electric cars by the second decade of the next millenium? Possible. An entire region that is independent of oil, coal, or uranium? A city surrounded by forests and filled with the plants of every species—the same plants now being poisoned by the pollution in the air? The value of full-scale development of photovoltaics and renewable technology is immeasurable in terms of dollars.

Nevertheless, financial considerations remain primary. And it is highly likely that PV electricity will be competitive with all other sources within five to eight years. It is also highly likely that more than one major utility will become involved in distributing and installing PV systems. And it is conceivable that the entry of a few utilities into the PV-installation business could result in a stampede—they'll all do it. Given the competitive implications of lower cost electricity on the location of commercial enterprises—factories, office buildings, and so on—few utilities will be able to ignore photovoltaics and their companion renewables.

If the scenario outlined for Southern California Edison occurred nationwide, we would see some profound changes indeed. The coal industry would stabilize in its growth rate and probably begin a long slow decline. Similarly, domestic oil production and the importation of oil would decline. The current trend of refinery closings in the United States—often linked to lower refining costs overseas—would continue until an oil refinery was a rare industrial activity. Builders of coal- and oil-fired power plants would be looking for work, possibly shifting their efforts towards the construction of new photovoltaic-, wind-, water-, and wood-power projects. And the "watershed" effect of rapid development in photovoltaics would probably cause a raft of new developments, and attendant impacts, in all other forms of renewable energy.

Environmentally, we would witness a steady decrease in the acid rain caused by the burning of coal. We would see a decrease in the horrific environmental destruction caused by tunnel and strip mining. Within decades fewer tankers would be crossing the oceans; thus the risk of oil spills and further damage to an already polluted sea would diminish. In three to five decades, maybe sooner, we would see a dramatic decline in air pollution and a parallel improvement in the health of forests and other biotic communities. And, although it is difficult to predict such an indirect result, it is conceivable that the development of renewable energy would stimulate us to value reforestation more highly.

Currently, the planet is losing its forested areas at a frightening pace, particularly in tropical areas. This loss in our oxygen-producing forests is exacerbating the greenhouse effect—it means that our dioxide-recycling species are diminishing. Reforestation is the only true antidote to the buildup of carbon dioxide in the atmosphere. Paradoxically, using wood as a basic fuel as well as a source of basic chemicals for plastics and pulp for papermaking could increase the value of reforestation. As oil becomes more expensive, it is probable that the long-distance transport of wood will become less economically feasible. As a result, there may be growing pressure to expand forested areas and restore destroyed forests to bring wood closer to its point of use. It is conceivable that reforestation may become a major world effort within the next twenty years, as a solution both to the problems of environmental pollution and the dwindling of nonrenewable energy sources.

The impact of photovoltaic technology on a farm perhaps characterizes its impact on society at large. The contemporary American farm, whether a corporate enterprise or a family one many generations old, has become a major consumer of energy. In most cases, where farms can produce their own energy by gas or diesel generator, the effort has proved more expensive than importing oil and electricity—or so farmers have tended to think. In any case, the farm is now dependent on oil-based fertilizers, pesticides, and fuels as well as utility-generated electricity—or farm-generated electricity. Thus, the American farm, while a phenomenal producer, is also a monocultural food factory resting to a great degree on outside energy, outside technology, and outside investment.

There is now a growing movement throughout farming regions of the United States toward organic farming and a diverse multi-crop growing strategy. Although the movement remains small, it is growing in influence, especially in those farming communities that have become most dependent upon government programs and outside sources of energy. Typically, the modern large-scale organic farm is capable of producing about the same amount as its chemically fueled counterpart but with a fraction of the fertilizer and pesticide costs. As yet the energy component of the organic-farming movement is not a centerpiece. Instead, attention remains focused, as it should be, on crops and livestock management. But as photovoltaic and other renewable-energy system prices drop we may see a sudden spurt of interest from the farming community.

The totally self-sustaining organic farm receiving little outside input, just normal financing and machinery, is technically feasible. It may become an economic necessity in the next ten years, representing one of the few means for farmers to reduce costs substantially. The likelihood of rising prices—of fuel and farm implements, of utility electricity, and fertilizer—coupled with ongoing financial problems and various regional problems such as the loss of topsoil and the decline in aquifers and water quality may result in a sweeping reform of the entire farm economy, and the technology of farming along with it. Practically the same factors that led to a similar period of reform in the 1930s are now in place.

Photovoltaic water-pumping systems are already used on many farms. In many areas they are more dependable than windmills. Small methane digesters are common in many parts of the world and could generate more than sufficient methane gas for farm activities requiring gaseous fuel. For farms with the proper feedstock, ethanol production, with animal feed a by-product, is quite feasible, and could result in an excellent vehicle fuel. Open prairie, coastal, and foothill farms often have enough wind power passing over the fields not only to supply their own needs but to generate a surplus. In wetter regions, such as the foothills of the Berkshires in Massachusetts or the Cascade range in Oregon, farms could receive a considerable amount of energy from hydroelectric generators either in-stream or at a dam—the pond can become a resource unto itself. In all such areas, the organic farm often requires a network of windrows and hedges that act as windbreaks and habitats for beneficial insects and birds. Windrows can be productive woodlots—sources of wood for farms as well as a potential crop to be sold to city customers, who, having converted to solar, would of course need a little wood every winter.

In all these circumstances, photovoltaics could provide anywhere from 20 percent to more than 85 percent of the farm's total energy needs. Since many farm machines—notably dairy machines—now operate with small electric motors, the transition to PVs would not be difficult. And many field machines are used only intermittently and only then in sunshine, so a photovoltaic-powered fleet of farm implements, some with battery storage, is also a possibility. Practically all renewable sources are already cheaper than conventional sources for most purposes in most of the country. Photovoltaics are the key.

The invention of new tools is an activity bound to reflect the changing social context in which the invention occurs. Each influences the other: the tool causes social change and the social change causes the tool. Our time has been a time of specialists, highly trained experts who know everything there is to know about particular professions, technologies, processes, or events. And not just our people but our institutions and technology have become specialized. Every *single* thing has had only one function to the exclusion of all others. As a direct result of the environmental movement and the new awareness it has fostered, many people now realize, in very pragmatic terms, that we cannot do just one thing in isolation, and that everything we do has intended and unintended results—this goes with the territory of change. The very idea of "cogeneration" was a major breakthrough in awareness for many in the energy industry. In many parts of the world cogeneration had been commonplace, but in much of the United States this old idea had an almost revolutionary implication. The machine that symbolized the age of the specialist, the nuclear power plant, with its army of extremely highly trained technicians and its millions of BTUs per hour streaming forth as "waste" heat, only did one thing. If there is one tool that will someday be seen as typifying the new age, whatever that age might be called, it ought to be the photovoltaic cell. And if one idea could characterize the new age it would be that of using a diversity of energy sources.

Utilities are increasingly moving towards a greater diversity of energy sources. Furthermore, all corporations involved in the energy business are ever more concerned not only about diversity in source of supply and technology but about minimizing environmental risk—inherently a more generalist perspective.

Diversity and interdependence are intrinsic characteristics of a sun-based economy, presuming that all potential renewable energy sources are developed. And since photovoltaics represent the most widely applicable means of gathering solar energy, the development of PV technology will probably initiate a coevolutionary cycle—more diverse sources and types of photovoltaic systems will in turn change our view of how energy occurs. As our view of energy changes, so also will the technology change.

The organic farm, as opposed to the monocultural, or single-crop, farm, must be a diverse biotic community if it is to be successful. It must also allow the coexistence of wild and domestic life: carefully planted and tended crops living in a larger matrix of wild hedgerows and windrows of trees. In the same way, many utilities are now relying on a combination of highly controlled precision machines and a diversity of renewable resources that might be technically predictable insofar as their performance is concerned but are totally unpredictable in output, since they are reliant upon the climate. Farmers working an organic farm cannot risk monoculture; rather they must plant diversely and secure energy from diverse sources. Increasingly, utility managers must do the same thing. This approach to energy inevitably leads to a much subtler and more intricate view of the environment, of Earth. Indeed, it leads to faith in the energetic processes of the universe.

This is not to suggest that photovoltaics are some miraculous tool that will electrify us with universal wisdom. PVs are, after all, just a simple tool. But they are also a mirror—both in their immediate function and in the way they are used, they reflect our perceptions of energy, matter, and value. And, like it or not, America and to some extent the world in the late twentieth century has been heavily infused with a faith in science and technology. Millions of people *want* to believe that a specific technology will somehow change their lives for the better. Considering all the benign and quite remarkable inventions we have seen since the wondrous electric light came on the scene, this faith is understandable. Given this tendency towards elevating a technological creation to the status of an icon, and given the obvious quality of the photovoltaic cell and its implications, we may be looking forward to a technological *and* cultural revolution of profound import. In this context, it is important to keep in mind that more than half the world has no electricity and none of its attendant cultural and industrial effects, and that if the whole world is to be electrified, photovoltaics are almost certainly going to be the technological agent of that change.

People living in the world's industrialized areas will probably "convert" to renewable energy and photovoltaics over the next thirty to forty years. But those living in the world's vast nonelectrified areas will begin their process of industrialization—to whatever extent it occurs—with renewables, especially PVs. There is simply no way that this development cannot result in a greater awareness of the sun, wind, rain, and seasons. Regardless of the local religion, the development of photovoltaic electricity will cause a realignment of cultural and spiritual values. A local culture will suddenly be tied into international, or at least regional, communications networks. It will be possible to refrigerate food and medicine, but perhaps more important, though not as immediately apparent, will be the transition from a society that has only a minimal energy "income" to one that is comparatively wealthy in energy. And unlike cultures that have been industrialized for decades, those newly electrified will not pay the horrendous environmental and political costs associated with coal and oil development. Indeed, electricity will occur not by an ethic of control and domination but as a simple transaction involving a precise study of the energy present in a particular place.

Many of the cultural and economic dislocations common in the world today are the direct result of the vast disparity between the industrialized haves and undeveloped have-nots. For more than a century, the developed nations have used wars, economic colonialism, covert support of fascist regimes, and all manner of marketing ploys to sustain a high level of industrialization at the expense of less developed regions. Predictably, the result has been a degree of resentment within less developed regions toward more developed regions. This pattern has, and is, occurring across regional and continental boundaries, and between small villages and big cities that otherwise speak the same language. Energy is the basic economic element of industrialization, and its distribution is often the root of disputes, resentments, and wars.

The spread of photovoltaic and renewable technologies across the planet will not eliminate war or conflict, but it is quite likely that this single development, more than any other technology, will dramatically reduce the disparity between rich and poor, between industrialized and nonindustrialized. However, it may also set up a whole new pattern. Less developed countries will be capable of supporting a modicum of industry, and in many cases this will mean cheap labor *and* cheap electricity. As demonstrated by the recent shift of multinational corporations toward manufacturing operations in the Far East, there is no shortage of corporate entities—U.S., Japanese, or European—willing to take advantage of cheap labor and cheap power. Such moves could be characterized as "cheap shots," but they are nonetheless inevitable.

While the corporations, governments, and individuals that might be involved in a given technological transaction may have hidden agendas a mile long, they speak a language of machines that is rapidly becoming universal. English is the world's most widely used language, but the language of technology—its parts, logic, impacts, and costs—is even more universal. The experience of modern technology—from steamships to trains to cars to exotic new tools like semiconductors—is increasingly a global experience. Practically all cultures on Earth have gone through or will soon go through a sequence of social and economic changes that result from wave upon wave of new technology.

The use of oil, coal, and nuclear power, in that order, is a common experience shared by many cultures of the world. True, small groups of Indians in the southern mountains of Mexico do not know how a large steam-generating station operates, but they know that gasoline is a precious commodity of great value to those they may know, if not to them. In that way, the technology of fossil fuels is a world experience. But photovoltaic technology may become even more widespread.

Over the next five decades, the growth of a sun-based economy is likely to result in a worldwide familiarity with technology that is intrinsically in tune with natural energy flows. Economic shifts and probable social disruptions aside, this experience should result in a worldwide awareness of our reliance, as species on the third planet from the sun, upon the ebb and flow of universal energies. In essence, the next half-century could bring the planet's first nearly total technological experience. During that time, managers of corporations—oil companies and utilities—organic farmers in the United States and Argentina, villagers in Ethiopia, comrades in

Cuba, and suburban residents of Hollywood might all come to
share a common perception of energy and the technology needed
to capture some of it.

Many observers who have studied the dynamics of rapid population growth in the less developed countries have concluded that,
apart from often Draconian birth control measures, the only truly
effective means of limiting population is increasing the standard of
living. Developing local electricity can increase the standard of living more than any other single act. If the means of electrification is
also inherently decentralized and reliant upon natural energy flows,
then a strong connection is established between improvement in the
quality of life and the development of technology that is inherently
in tune with local energy income.

Admittedly, this relationship is somewhat speculative, and it
may be played out in a thousand variations, but the basic pattern is
plausible. Solar electricity in a place results in an improvement in
the quality of life: the birth rate drops; the local population comes
to perceive energy as a function of the environment, *as it is;* the
region becomes linked with the world's extensive communications
network; and the population adopts the perceptual framework
shared by practically the entire planet.

Albert Einstein gave us two theories, relativity and photovoltaic. Development of the first led to explorations in the realm of
atomic particles, to nuclear power plants, and to the most horrible
weapon ever created. But those explorations also set the stage for
the development of the second theory, and the creation of objects
that perform extraordinarily elemental functions—semiconductors
and photovoltaics. In all our years of living with nuclear weapons,
there has been precious little mention of the horrific environmental
implications of nuclear war. In the last few years, various groups of
scientists, including groups under contract to the U.S. Department
of Defense, have clearly proven the thesis that even a "limited"
nuclear war would be tantamount to species suicide. Nuclear winter would not be caused by the severity of the explosions or their
radioactivity but by the dust raised and the smoke from subsequent
fires. This single thesis has, at least on paper, totally undercut the
belief, held by a shrinking but vocal military and political contin-
gent of hawks, that nuclear weapons are a valid tool of war. Within
the same time period, roughly 1983–1985, the nuclear power
industry has practically collapsed, at least in the United States.

And nearly simultaneously, the photovoltaic industry has appeared totally out of left field to become a serious entrant in the world energy business. One man, two theories written down almost eighty years ago, and two possibilities—species suicide or a radical economic transformation that would dramatically improve life for much of the world's population. Both possibilities are unprecedented, unparalleled, and staggering in their implications.

Bibliography

Books

DASMANN, RAYMOND F. *Environmental Conservation*, 5th ed. New York: Wiley, 1984.
An excellent source of information on general energy issues in their environmental context.

DAVIDSON, JOEL, AND KOMP, RICHARD. *The Solar Electric Home*. Ann Arbor, Mich.: Aatec, 1983.
A little funky in places but generally excellent on installing PV systems on small houses.

FLAVIN, CHRISTOPHER. *Electricity from Sunlight: The Future of Photovoltaics, Worldwatch Paper #52*. Washington, D.C.: Worldwatch Institute, 1982.

————, *Nuclear Power: The Market Test, Worldwatch Paper #57*. Washington, D.C.: Worldwatch Institute, 1983.

————, *Electricity's Future: The Shift to Efficiency and Small Scale Power, Worldwatch Paper # 61*. Washington, D.C.: Worldwatch Institute, 1984.
These three small booklets cover the energy business in the United States in the mid-eighties in a readable way.

HENDERSON, HAZEL. *The Politics of the Solar Age*. New York: Doubleday, 1981.
Not a light read. Dense and conceptually complex but one of the best and most scholarly outlines of the probable oncoming solar age.

KOMP, RICHARD. *Practical Photovoltaics*. Ann Arbor, Mich.: Aatec, 1983.
A good outline of photovoltaic manufacturing technology from an elemental standpoint. Shows how to make your own PVs from raw cells. Rough on sophisticated mass manufacturing technology.

LOVINS, AMORY. *Soft Energy Paths*. New York: Harper & Row, 1977.
Given recent developments in photovoltaics and other energy technology, this book is somewhat dated. The "alternative" is even more viable now. But this work redefined the energy issue by asking the right questions.

MAYCOCK, PAUL, AND STIREWALT, EDWARD. *Photovoltaics*. Andover, Mass.: Brick House, 1981.
Now somewhat dated but an excellent overview of the use and potential of the technology.

221

Government Publications

OFFICE OF SOLAR ELECTRIC TECHNOLOGIES. *Five Year Research Plan 1984–1988*. Washington, D.C.: U.S. Department of Energy, 1983 (DOE/CE-0072).

RASHKIN, SAMUEL. *Photovoltaic User Guide*. Sacramento: California Energy Commission, 1983.
A good workbook for calculating the size and finances of a photovoltaic system.

SOLAR ENERGY RESEARCH INSTITUTE, Jet Propulsion Laboratory. *Photovoltaic Energy Systems*. Washington, D.C.: U.S. Department of Energy, 1983 (DOE/CE-0033/2).
A dated summary of research activity in PV technology in the United States. But if you want to know who's doing PV research, this is the sourcebook. Contains short abstracts on every imaginable aspect of PV technology.

Magazines and Newsletters

Solar Age. Harrisville, New Hampshire 03450.
Does not focus on PVs but often includes excellent articles on PV technology. Provides an overview of some PV technology and much solar-water and space-heating technology.

Photovoltaics International. 999 18th Street, Suite 1000, Denver, Colorado 80202.
The first and still most authoritative magazine on PVs worldwide. A year's subscription will put you up to date each month.

Photovoltaic News (a newsletter). Paul D. Maycock, 2401 Childs Lane, Alexandria, Virginia 22308.
Mr. Maycock has followed the PV industry from the beginning and knows the technology, markets, and potential perhaps better than anyone. Very timely on the latest fast-breaking developments.

Other Sources

Also consulted in the preparation of this book was a wide range of photovoltaic-company literature, utility-company publications, state papers and brochures, federal government energy publications, and publications of the Solar Energy Research Institute. Because the technology is so new and so little understood, most manufacturers produce unusually detailed and informative literature on their products. ARCO Solar is perhaps the most informative, followed by Mobil Solar Energy Corporation.

Some states, notably Massachusetts and California, are very supportive of photovoltaic industries and have published various documents on the technology and its regional use. Also, some utilities now publish consumer information on conservation and solar technology; a few publish information on photovoltaics.

Index